T0353472

Certifiable Software Applications 2

I thank my wife Nadège and my children
Geoffrey, Adrien, Marie and Jeanne for their love and support.

Certifiable Software Applications 2

Applications 2

Support Processes

Jean-Louis Boulanger

ELSEVIER

British Library Cataloguing-in-Publication Data
A CIP record for this book is available from the British Library
Library of Congress Cataloging in Publication Data
A catalog record for this book is available from the Library of Congress
ISBN 978-1-78548-118-5

Printed and bound in the UK and US

Contents

Introduction

This introduction is shared across the different volumes of this series on the development of *certifiable* software applications.

Developing a software application is a difficult process that requires teamwork. The complexity of software applications is ever increasing and the amount has grown from a few tens of thousands to a few million. In order to be able to manage this complexity, development teams are of significant importance. The involvement of development teams in a software application, the internationalization of companies for a better distribution of work teams (multisite companies, use of outsourcing, etc.) – all these factors combined make it difficult to manage the complexity of a software application.

The complexity of developing a software application is further intensified by the race to obsolescence. The obsolescence of the hardware components entails the implementation of specific strategies (saving equipment, repository of tool sources, etc.) and mastering reproducibility and maintainability of the software application.

Another challenge is the requirement to demonstrate the safety of a software application. The demonstration of safety relies on the development of specific techniques (diversity, redundancy, fault tolerance, etc.) and/or controlling defects in the software application.

Even though the relationships related to systems and hardware architectures are introduced in these volumes, only the software aspect shall be discussed in detail [BOU 09a].

This book series is a concrete presentation of the development of a critical software application. This approach is based on quality assurance as defined in ISO 9001 [ISO 08] and various industry standards such as DO 178 (aeronautics), IEC 61508 (programmable system), CENELEC 50128 (railway), ISO 26262 (automotive) and IEC 880 (nuclear). It must be noted that this book series is only a complement to other existing books such as the one written by Ian Sommerville [SOM 07].

Reader's guide

Volume 1 [BOU 16] is dedicated to the establishment of quality assurance and safety assurance. The concept of a software application and the relationship with the system approach are addressed here. This chapter, therefore, discusses the fundamentals including the management of requirements.

Volume 2 describes the support processes, such as qualification tools, configuration management, verification and validation. Volume 2 is essential to understand what is necessary to develop a certifiable software application.

Volume 3 [BOU 17a] describes all the activities to be performed in the downward phase of the V cycle to produce a version of the software application. Activities such as specification, the establishment of an architecture and design of a software application are discussed here. This volume concludes with the presentation of production code of software application.

Volume 4 [BOU 17b] discusses the ascending phase of the V cycle along with a description of various stages of testing (unit tests, modular tests, component testing, integration tests and testing of the entire software) and various other associated tests. All these activities lead to the production of a version of the software application.

Acknowledgments

This book is a compilation of all my work carried out with the manufacturers to implement systems that are safe and secure for people.

Realization of a Software Application

1.1. Introduction

A software application is an element of a more complex set (system, subsystem, equipment) as shown in Figure 1.1. Recall that a software application is directly linked to equipment and in the absence of hardware architecture there can be no software application.

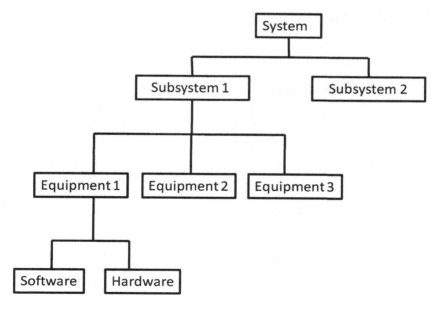

Figure 1.1. *Architecture: from system to software*

The realization process of a software application should take into account several factors: type of application, application size, criticality, deadlines, etc.

As discussed in Chapter 1 of Volume 1 [BOU 16], the need to realize (see Figure 1.2) a software application is related to two situations; in the first case, it is required to realize a software application of the non-integrated type (desktop application, compiler, simulator, testing environment, etc.), and the second case is related to the realization of a system, subsystem or equipment, and thus the need to realize an embedded software application.

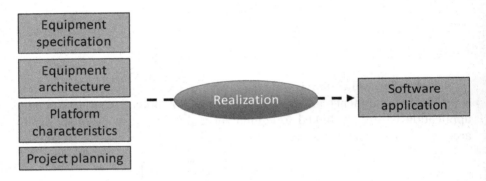

Figure 1.2. *Realization of an application*

This first distinction (nonintegrated vs. embedded) is important because the embedded environment is dependent on its execution platform (see Figure 1.3) and the realization process must take into account the realization schedule of the support system.

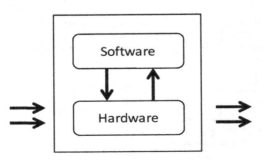

Figure 1.3. *Software in equipment*

In [BOU 09a, BOU 11a], we presented real examples of safe architectures and related operating constraints. These constraints can orient the realization process of the software application.

For the non-integrated application, the execution platform is a PC or Mac type machine and the testing availability constraints are weaker. However, the problem of the definition of the target machine is more difficult:

– which operation system (OS) version (major version + patches – which patches and in what order);

– what are the libraries used and what version (it is currently very difficult to produce a static executable for new OS);

– what type of processor (single core, multicore, multithreaded application, etc.);

– what kind of hardware (video card, memory, etc.)?

In Volume 1 [BOU 16], we discussed the fact that a software application can be configured by data. Thus, two processes (see Figure 1.4) are to be implemented for the realization of a software application.

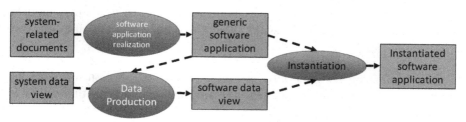

Figure 1.4. *Instantiated software application*

The first process that aims to realize the software application is called generic, and the second process aims to develop the configuration process. The configuration process is designed based on the knowledge of the generic software application. This process comprises the realization of the settings means and the definition of the instantiation process of the generic software application for a configuration.

The realization of a software application requires the definition of a strategy that is to be formalized in a software quality assurance plan (SQAP). This realization strategy must be within the context of a system's development.

1.2. What is software?

The element called "software" is a set of computing/processing elements executed on a hardware architecture that can render services associated with equipment (see Figure 1.1).

In this book, we will look at the software aspects, hence the problem of defining software (see definition 1.1). This definition is somewhat different from that of ISO 90003:2004 [ISO 04].

DEFINITION 1.1.– APPLICATION SOFTWARE: *A set of programs, methods and rules and optionally documentation relating to the operation of information processing.*

Definition 1.1 makes no distinction between the means (methods, processes, tools, etc.) required to perform the software application, the products issued from the development (documents, test results, models, sources, test scenarios, test results, specific tools, etc.) and the software application itself.

This definition is generally associated with the notion of software application. The notion of software is being associated with the notion of executable.

1.3. Software within a system

For a non-integrated application, the hardware constraints are defined in the beginning of the project but there is little constraint on the software application's realization process.

In the context of a system's realization and therefore of an embedded software application, the realization of the software application should be seen in a more complex assembly that may require synchronization between different processes and the production of several versions.

Figure 1.5 shows an example of the relationship between the different realization tasks. The solid arrows indicate the realization inputs. The dotted arrows indicate versions that are needed to develop the integrations. Note that the three realization processes are parallelized but must be synchronized, hence the need to produce intermediate versions.

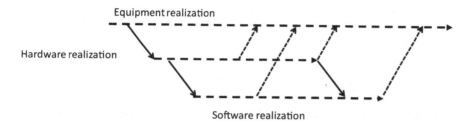

Figure 1.5. *Example of dependency between the realization processes*

Figure 1.6 demonstrates the relationship between the hardware and software realization. The hardware specification is an input for the software and hardware is an input for the software's integration and validation.

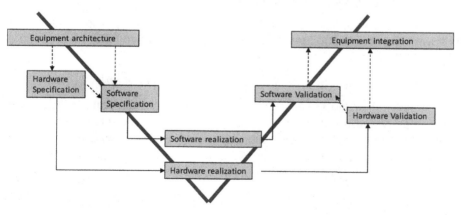

Figure 1.6. *Relation between hardware and software*

The realization process of an application is constrained by the overall needs that must be taken into account. We can have an impact on the size of the team (to best meet the deadlines), the supply of different versions with perimeters that are defined in advance or on the risks taken to anticipate the realization on the basis of a non-finalized specification need.

1.4. Different types of software applications

The objective of this section is to recall the different types of software that can be realized in order to better understand the constraints on the development process.

1.4.1. *Different types of software*

As part of the realization of a reliable critical application, software applications to be produced may be of different types:

– *application (or operational) software*: These are embedded within a device. They are part of the final system. They are delivered to a customer as part of a project and/or product. Note that the external use test benches are in this category.

There are two subtypes of application software:

- *configurable applications*: A dataset enables the specialization of the software for a specific use (see Figure 1.3 and Chapter 2 of Volume 1 [BOU 16]),

    - *non-configurable applications (they are less common)*;

– *development tools*: These tools concern software applications internal to the company and not delivered to the customer; they are intended to aid the realization (editor, IDE, code generator, compiler, charger, etc.) in a broad sense, including tests (testing environment, internal bench testing, etc.);

– *"offline" tools*: This latter category of software allows the preparation of elements, such as data to be integrated in the final software application.

They are part of the final application but are not performed on the equipment. They can be delivered or not to the customer.

1.4.2. *Different uses*

Definition 1.1 demonstrates the concept of software, but it should be noted that there are several types of software:

– *operational software*: any software delivered to external customers as part of a program or product. External use test benches fall into this category;

– *demonstrator*: software used by an external client to refine his expression of needs and measure the potential level of service provided. These programs are not aimed for an operational use;

– *development tool*: internal software not delivered to an external client, which aims to aid in the realization in the broad sense (editor, tool-chain, etc.), including testing and integration;

– *model*: non-supplied internal study software used to verify a theory, algorithm or the feasibility of the technique (e.g. simulation) without a completion or result target.

1.5. Lifecycle

As discussed earlier, it is preferable to speak of the realization and not the development of a software application. The realization of a software application contains development activities as well as verification, validation, production, deployment and maintenance.

The realization process of a software application requires the implementation of different stages, activities and resources. This is why it is necessary to formalize it in the form of a lifecycle.

As shown in Figure 1.7, there are several cycles ((a) V cycle, (b) cascade cycle, (c) spiral cycle, etc.) for carrying out a generic software application, but the recommended cycle by different standards (CENELEC 50128, IEC 61508 and ISO 26262) remains the V cycle (see Figure 1.8).

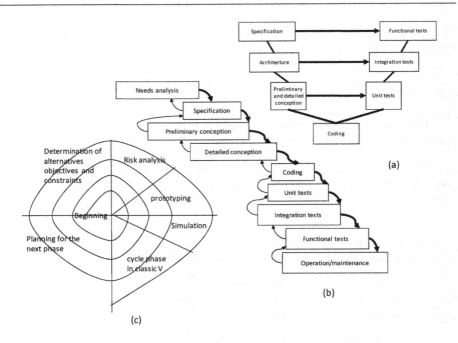

Figure 1.7. *Different cycles of software realization*

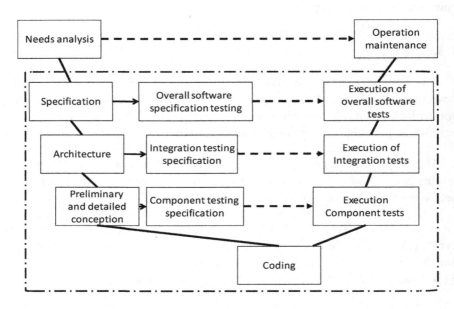

Figure 1.8. *V cycle*

Finally, a realization cycle must be defined and the different aspects must be controlled such as the application development cycle, managing requirements traceability, change management, configuration management, tool management, etc.

1.6. Choice of the software application development strategy

The drafting of the SQAP will be done after the establishment of the realization process of the software application; it must take into account the following:

– *development context*: deadlines, team size, project complexity, project size, reuse rate, use of COTS (commercial off-the-shelf), safety levels, number of innovations, etc;

– *development cycle*: Based on the context and processes defined in the company's quality assurance manual, we can select a development cycle. The reference cycle may be amended – through derogation – to take the context into account;

– the impact of the lifecycle on the product.

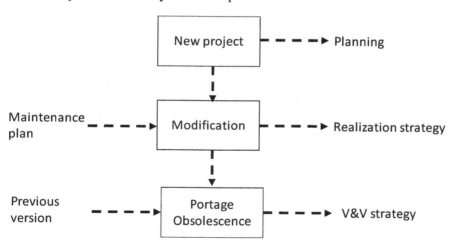

Figure 1.9. *Different types of development*

The "development context" of the software application targets the type of development of the final product. The concept of software development context is available in terms of:

– *type of process* (see Figure 1.9): new software, delivery, maintenance, reuse, product line, using COTS, etc.;

– *embedded or not*: the embedded software must meet specific technical features, and the non-integrated application should run on all machines of a given type (PC under Windows X);

– *final usage*: software, layout, prototype.

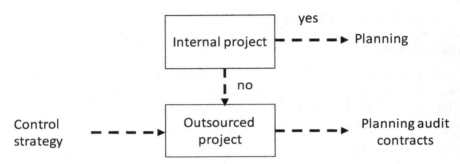

Figure 1.10. *Internal versus outsourced*

Figure 1.10 shows that the project can be done internally or can be outsourced. In case of outsourcing, it is necessary to check that the realized work complies with the safety objectives; to do this, it is necessary to set up audits. As shown in Figure 1.11, it is possible to set up three audits to monitor the realization process.

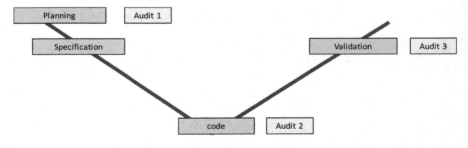

Figure 1.11. *Audit*

1.7. Conclusion

The objective of this chapter was to present a set of concepts related to the realization of a software application. It is essential to define the objective of the ongoing development (new software application, adaptation, delivery, adding of functionality, defect correction, etc.) and on the basis of this objective to identify the realization process to set up. This process will be related to the resources, and depending on the complexity and the organizational level of safety, the activities to be realized and tools will be adapted.

The SQAP will identify the objectives, means (human resources, tools, etc.), deadlines and activities to realize.

In the case of modifying an existing software application, it will be necessary to take into account two specific stages: the maintenance (Chapter 9) and deployment phases (Chapter 10).

1.8. Appendix A – structure of an SQAP

The SQAP must contain the elements that are described later in this section. The SQAP is divided into several documents, as shown in Figure 1.12.

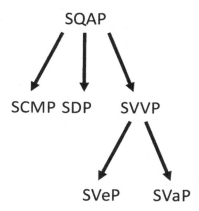

Figure 1.12. *Hierarchy of plans*

The topics to be addressed are as follows:

– *Section 1*: includes identification of the safety level and the applicable standards and mandatory regulations. After we identified the safety integrity level, the purpose of this section is to identify the set of standards and regulations to follow during the realization of the software. It is necessary to identify the titles, references and versions of these documents. We find the standards in this section for quality: ISO 9001: 2015, ISO 90003 and for ls DO 178: x, 61508: 20xx, ISO 26262, CENELEC 50128: 20xx, the IEC 62279: 20xx standards, etc.

– *Section 2*: consists of project organization (the part relating to software), demonstration of independence and justification of skills (it can rely on a process that is local to the project and management of the company's HR).

– *Section 3*: presents an overview of the scope of the realized software(s).

– *Section 4*: includes a presentation of the management and quality control (metrics, checkpoints, audit, etc.).

– *Section 5*: gives a presentation software development cycle (V cycle, etc.) of each phase. For each one, a subsection should describe the input elements, output elements, activities to realize, human and technical resources (tools, test environments, laboratories, etc.) and the criteria for acceptance and the end of phase control.

– *Section 6*: a detailed presentation of the configuration management (tool, procedure, version identification, identification of elements to manage, etc.). It will be necessary to explain how the software version sheet is produced.

– *Section 7*: includes a presentation of the error management process, amendment and correction requests.

– *Section 8*: a presentation of the tool management process (identification, configuration management, etc.) and particularly the management of tool qualification are discussed.

– *Section 9*: there must be a list of documents to be produced during the realization of the software.

– *Section 10*: it is necessary to demonstrate compliance with the standards identified in Section 1, and more particularly with the CENELEC standard 50128 (or IEC 62279). Compliance with the CENELEC EN 50128 standard must not only be based on the tables at the end of Chapter 6 but on the entire standard. Indeed, the body of the standard is normative and some subjects are not treated in Table A.x. For example in the 2001 version, test coverage is not treated by an A.x table but with a phrase in the body of the document. For the 2011 version, it is the tool qualification that is not treated by an A.x table.

2

Quality Assurance Implementation

2.1. Introduction

In Volume 1 [BOU 16] we discussed the need to control quality and in order to do so, it is possible to implement a quality approach at the company level through ISO 9001:2015 [ISO 15], with the Capability Maturity Model for Integration (CMMi)[1] or Software Process Improvement and Capability Determination (SPICE) [ISO 04].

Whatever the implemented approach, it is first necessary to establish a quality assurance that is characterized by the creation of a document repository and the establishment of an organization.

As shown in Figure 2.1, the quality management system (QMS) requires the establishment of a document repository and is generally composed of a quality assurance manual (QAM), a set of procedures describing the activity to be realized, a set of guidelines and a set of templates to produce.

2.2. Quality management system

A QMS must include all activities of the company; it is not uncommon to see an ISO 9001 certified company having no procedure on the

---

1 CMMi is a maturity model dedicated to the software industry, which is a set of good practices to implement in development projects. For more information, see the *Software Engineering Institute* website: www.sei.cmu.edu/cmmi.

development of a software application. For software development, the minimum process to implement is ISO 9001 through its specialization, ISO 90003, and then a standard that is a superset of ISO 9001 + ISO 90003.

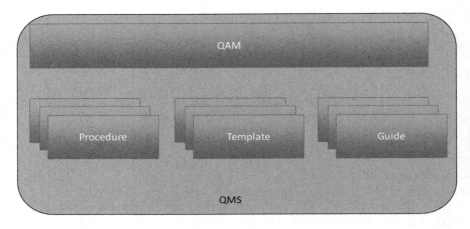

Figure 2.1. *Quality management system*

The QAM must cover all the business processes for the realization of a software application including all stages (from the specification to the delivery of the software application) of the realization cycle.

For each step of the realization cycle, it is necessary to have:

– a procedure that describes activities to realize, the documents to produce and those in charge of realizing the activities;

– a set of guidelines allowing the limiting of the methods' field of use (a UML[2] guide [OMG 11, ROQ 07] will aim to explain how to realize a model and how to read it);

– a set of plan types that help in the document production by defining a minimum content.

Guidelines must capture the knowledge and the company's experience feedback, therefore allowing for the training of new company members quickly. We must remember that quality must be preestablished and systematic.

---

2 To know more, see the OMG website: www.omg.org/.

We have a controlled and accepted quality standard that exists and which is applied regularly. A good QMS must be accepted by the people of the company.

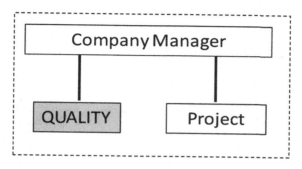

Figure 2.2. *Organization*

Although quality assurance is done through the construction and operational maintenance of the QMS and associated means, it is also necessary to carry out a quality control. The quality control of a software application requires a dual competence: a knowledge of the quality and knowledge of the realization of a software application in order to best interact with the teams that are responsible for implementation.

As shown in Figure 2.2, within the company's organization, it is necessary to have a department (or service) dedicated to quality that covers both the quality of company and the quality of software application. The organization and mastery of competencies will be discussed in Chapter 5.

2.3. Characterization of a stage

A stage of the realization cycle (see Figure 2.3) is characterized by the input documents, output documents and job procedures and/or guidelines for the realization of activities.

In the following, we will describe, in addition to the input and output, the objectives and expectations associated with each stage of the realization.

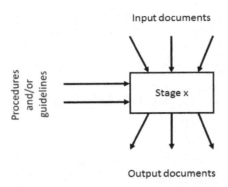

Figure 2.3. *Description of a stage*

2.4. Process

As shown in Figure 2.4, the realization of a software application may follow a cycle in V. The V cycle introduces two branches: the descending branch that supports the design and the ascending branch that supports the V&V activities.

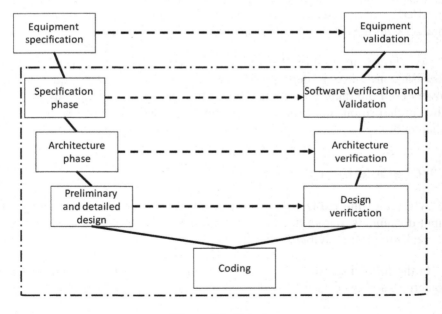

Figure 2.4. *V cycle*

2.5. Input elements

2.5.1. *Need identification*

In order to start the realization of the software application, it is necessary to have some elements that come from the design of the system (see Figure 1.6 and more specifically Figure 2.5): the equipment's specification, the equipment's architecture and the specifications of hardware.

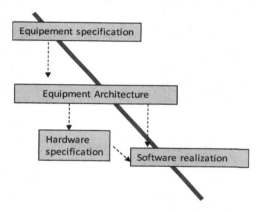

Figure 2.5. *The software application's realization inputs*

We must complete the systems design elements with the safety analysis results, which are formalized in the form of safety requirements (see Figure 2.6).

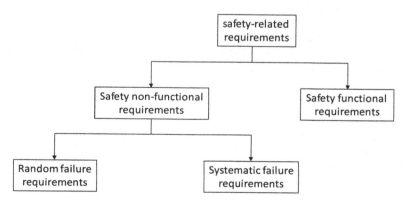

Figure 2.6. *Safety requirements*

2.5.2. *Need specification*

In order to realize software, it is necessary to have a description of the need at the higher level (system, subsystem and equipment). This specification should identify the software environment (hardware architecture, etc.) and interfaces to consider.

2.5.3. *Specification of safety requirements*

"System" safety studies (preliminary risk analysis, interfaces safety hazard analysis, system safety hazard analysis, operational safety hazard analysis, etc.) must exist and should identify safety requirements. On this basis, we must be able to identify the requirements that are applicable to the software application.

2.6. Descriptions of the realization stages

Within the framework of this section, we describe the different stages of a realization cycle of software application. We take the V realization cycle as our reference as it remains the cycle that is used throughout different standards. The following sections describe the points that will be detailed for each stage.

2.6.1. *Planning of activities*

2.6.1.1. *Objective*

The objective of this stage is to identify the resources (human, tools, etc.), the time required, the responsibilities and the elements to produce during the production of software application.

2.6.1.2. *Inputs*

– QAM.

– Applicable standards depending on the field (CEI 61508, DO 178, CENELEC EN 50128, EN 50155, ISO 26262) and the type of product.

2.6.1.3. *Procedures and applicable guides*

– The company's applicable quality procedures for a software applications development.

– Templates of the software plans: SQAP, SCMP, SVVP (SVeP, SVaP), etc.

– Methodological guides.

2.6.1.4. *Outputs*

– Software quality assurance plan (SQAP).

– Software configuration management plan (SCMP).

– Software verification plan (SVeP).

– Software validation plan (SVaP).

2.6.1.5. *Description*

The planning stage is aimed at developing plans that will be implemented to realize the software application. Planning should cover four areas:

– *The software application's quality management*: This requires defining the means that should be implemented for the realization of a software application. The means are human and material resources, means in terms of methods and processes and tools.

– *The software configuration's management*: We must be able to know at all times the list of items produced in the framework of the realization of the software application and the associated versions. It must be indicated that the sources and the executable generation process are just a few elements from the software's realization and that we must not forget all the produced documentation (plans, specifications, design documents, test records, verification documents, end of phase reports, etc.), the different scenarios and test results (UT, CT, IT and OST), the results of phase verification tools (coverage summary file, metrics summary file, code analyzers report, etc.).

– *Design management*: The lifecycle of the design of the software application has to be described along with every step that constitutes it. For each step, it is necessary to know the inputs and outputs, the implemented methods, the tools used and the verification objectives.

– *The management of the verification and validation*: The activities of verification and validation must be defined and positioned on the software's realization lifecycle. The organization and responsibilities of the V&V team must be clearly defined[3].

The SQAP is the first plan to be produced and on the basis of a lifecycle, the V cycle (see Figure 2.4) is generally used and defines phases to realize the software application. The SQAP must identify the human resources and responsibilities via an organization that must comply with rules of independence. Within the framework of Chapter 7, we will identify the needs for the organization and the mastery of competencies.

In view of the project's organization, the SQAP generally introduces the lifecycle and completely defines the design phases and requires (see Figure 2.7) a SCMP a software development plan (SDP), an SVeP and SVaP.

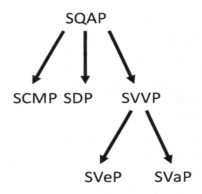

Figure 2.7. *Hierarchy of plans*

In order to achieve the above objectives, the SCMP is applicable to all the elements produced during the project. The SVeP describes the objectives and means of verification that are associated with each phase of the lifecycle, unit and integration testing (software/software and software/hardware). The

3 In view of the independence rules that are introduced by different standards (IEC 61508, DO 178, CENELEC EN 50128, ISO 26262, IEC 62279), people performing the verification may be in the same team or not as the people in charge of the validation. As part of this book, we consider that there is a V&V team.

SVaP describes the objectives and means for the final step, which is the software application's validation.

In some cases, the SVeP and SVaP are grouped in a verification and validation plan, which covers the verification of each phase of the lifecycle, unit testing, integration testing (software/software and software/hardware) and on target validation testing.

The development part of the software application (specification phase to the coding phase) can be described through a SDP, which will define the human resources, phases, methods, and elements to produce. This plan is then referenced by the SQAP.

2.6.2. Software application specifications

2.6.2.1. Objective

The software specification stage has a dual objective, the description of the need and the software application's validation preparation. The description of the need gives rise to a specification file of the software application. In order to realize the software application's validation, a specification document of software validation tests will describe all the tests that need to be performed.

2.6.2.2. Inputs

– System Requirement Specification (SyRS).

– System architecture description document (SyAD).

– SQAP.

– SVaP.

– SVeP.

– Project glossary (GL).

2.6.2.3. Applicable procedures and guidelines

– Templates for SwRS (Software Requirement Specification) and overall software test specification (OSTS) document.

– Methodological guide for the selection of OST (Overall Software Test).

– Guide to writing a SwRS.

– Guide to writing an OSTS.

– Modeling guide if necessary.

2.6.2.4. Outputs

– Software specification document (SwRS).

– OSTS document.

– Software specification verification report (SwS-VR).

– Updated project glossary (GL).

– Anomaly (if it occurred).

2.6.2.5. Description

From input higher level documents (SyRS, SyAD and GL), a stage consisting of acquiring the need must be implemented that should identify the scope, services and the requirements applicable to the software application. In terms of quality standards, a procedure must describe the process to follow in order to get the SwRs. One must at least have a standard SwRs plan. The specification stage of the software application is described in detail in Volume 3 [BOU 17a].

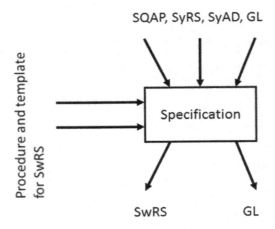

Figure 2.8. *Specification*

The SwRS template must describe the steps for realizing the SwRS and the means that must be implemented. If the specification of software application is based on a model, it is necessary to have a modeling guide that describes the semantics of the elements used for modeling, naming and decomposition rules and design rules that must be implemented during the model's realization.

Once the SwRS is available, it is possible to prepare the validation phase of the software application by developing the OSTS document. The methodology and means must be consistent with the SVaP. The implementation of the validation step is described in Volume 4 [BOU 17b].

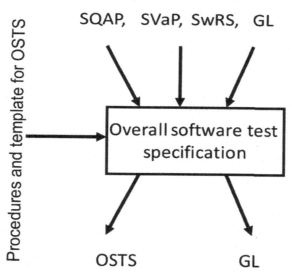

Figure 2.9. *Software's overall testing specification*

The software specification phase ends with a stage that verifies that it was correctly realized. To do this, the software's specification must be verified (consistency, completeness, correctness, etc.) and the software's overall testing specification should be verified as covering the overall specification of the software. All tests that must be performed are described in the SVeP and their results are formalized in the SwS-VR.

Figure 2.10 shows the verification phases (dashed arrows). We can see that the production of the specification of the software's overall testing is an overall verification.

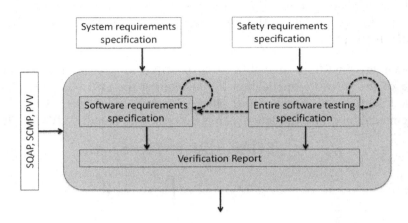

Figure 2.10. *Specification phase*

2.6.3. *Software application architecture*

2.6.3.1. *Objective*

The second phase of the V cycle for the realization of software is called architecture and design. It actually covers two stages (see Figure 2.11); the definition of architecture and its decomposition into components (see Volume 1 [BOU 16]). In addition, this phase of the lifecycle should allow the identification of integration testing. Integration testing should cover two topics, software/software integration testing (that allows the verification of software interfaces) and software/hardware integration testing (which focus on the verification of hardware interfaces).

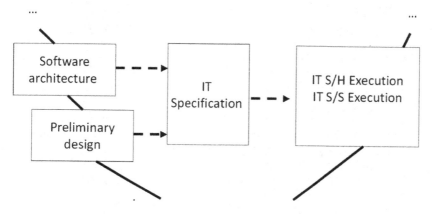

Figure 2.11. *Architecture and design phase*

2.6.3.2. *Inputs*

- SwDS.
- SQAP.
- SVeP.
- Project glossary (GL).

2.6.3.3. *Applicable procedures and guidelines*

- Templates for SwAD, software design document (SwDD) and SwITS.
- Modeling guide if necessary.
- Methodological guide for IT selection.
- SwAD writing guide.
- SwITS writing guide.
- SwDD writing guide.

2.6.3.4. *Outputs*

- SwAD.
- SwDD.
- Software/software integration test specification (S/S-ITS) document.

– Software/software integration test specification (S/H-ITS) document.

– Software architectural phase verification report (SwA-VR).

– Updated project glossary (GL).

– Anomaly (if it occurred).

2.6.3.5. *Description*

Once the software application specification is realized, it is possible to implement the architecture (see Figure 2.12). This architecture is designed to decompose the software application's components. The architecture must follow rules and be controlled; therefore, it will be essential to verify its complexity (number of interfaces, number of interconnections, number of components at each level, etc.).

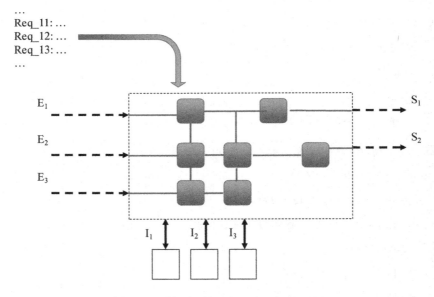

Figure 2.12. *Architecture requirements*

Figure 2.13 shows a software architecture of the railway type. There is a first layer that is in charge of managing the hardware aspects and execution (it may be an operating system, an execution loop, a sequencer, etc.). The second layer called middleware aims to manage communications. Then, we have a generic application and its settings (see Volume 1 [BOU 16]).

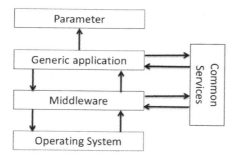

Figure 2.13. *Typical architecture*

As shown in Figure 2.14, the architecture and design phase has the planning documents, the software requirements specification and methodological guides as inputs. On this basis, the first activity consists of describing software interfaces to realize, the second consists of identifying the software architecture (SwAD), the third consists of realizing the design (SwDD) and finally, the integration tests have to be selected (ITS).

Integration testing aims to cover all of the software application's interfaces that consist of two types: the interfaces between software and software/hardware interfaces. The integration testing record will be split into two parts software/software ITS and software/hardware ITS.

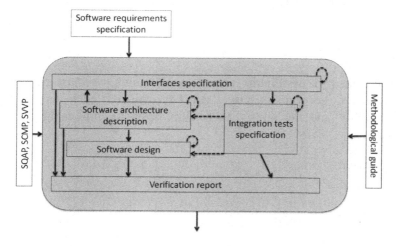

Figure 2.14. *Architecture and design phase activity*

The phase ends with the verification of all of the productions (dashed arrows in Figure 2.14). All verifications that must be performed are described in SVeP and their results are formalized in the SwA-VR.

2.6.4. Software application components design

2.6.4.1. Objective

As inputs to the components design (Figure 2.15), we must have a document describing the (SwADD/SwDD) architecture. However, the control of components design goes through the control of the design quality making it necessary to have a guide with a set of safety principles and a program guide.

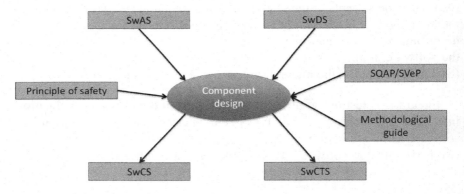

Figure 2.15. *Design process*

In the context of certifiable software applications, we must keep in mind that there are several objectives to be achieved such as testability, maintainability and the ability to perform tests to implement the safety demonstration.

2.6.4.2. Inputs

– SwAD.

– SQAP.

– SVeP.

– Project glossary (GL).

2.6.4.3. *Applicable procedures and guidelines*

– Templates for software component design (SwCD) and component testing specification (CTS).

– Methodological guide for the selection of CT.

– Guide to writing a SwCS.

– Guide to writing a SwCTS.

2.6.4.4. *Outputs*

– SwCD document.

– SwCTS document.

– Software design phase verification report (SwD-VR).

– Updated project glossary (GL).

– Anomaly (if it occurred).

2.6.4.5. *Description*

As inputs of the component design phase (see Figure 2.16), we have the software architecture and design and also the methodological documents such as a programming guide and/or guides describing the safety principles of a software application and design methodology.

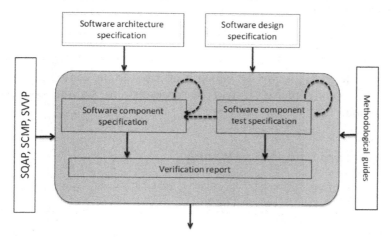

Figure 2.16. *Detailed design process*

The phase ends with the verification of all of the productions (dashed arrows in Figure 2.16). All testing to be performed is described in the SVeP and results are formalized in the SwD-VR.

2.6.5. Coding of the software application

2.6.5.1. Objective

The coding consists of transforming a component and algorithm into source code with the number of methodological guides as a constraint and an objective to do only what is required. If there are difficulties during the coding process requiring the completion of design documents, the person in charge of coding must report it and any realized choice must be formalized.

2.6.5.2. Inputs

– SwCD document.

– Project glossary (GL).

2.6.5.3. Applicable procedures and guidelines

– Coding guide for language XX (XX being C, ADA or other).

2.6.5.4. Outputs

– Managed code in configuration.

2.6.5.5. Description

This phase is carried out by the person in charge of coding. The code needs to conform to the SwCD, which is an input to the coding guide. In the end of the coding phase, it will be necessary to set the code in the configuration.

2.6.6. Software component testing

2.6.6.1. Objective

After the component coding step, we need to verify that the component works correctly.

To do this, we execute the previously defined component test. Component tests are executed by a tester.

In addition, the code coverage activity is done in this step to verify that all the code is executed. We also need to verify that all programming rules, coding style and metrics are verified by the code.

2.6.6.2. Inputs

- SVeP.
- Application code (SRC).
- Software component test specification (SwCTS).
- Software component test file (CTF).
- Project glossary (GL).

2.6.6.3. Applicable procedures and guidelines

- SwTCR type plan.
- SwTCR realization guide.

2.6.6.4. Outputs

- Software component test report (SwCTR).
- Anomaly (if it occurred).
- Coding phase verification report (SRC-VR).

2.6.6.5. Description

Figure 2.17 shows the activities associated with this phase. It is necessary to verify that the code conforms to the design and rules that were formalized in the methodological guidelines.

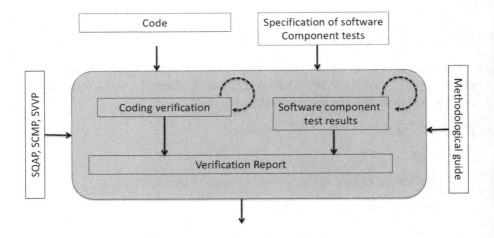

Figure 2.17. *Code verification and component testing process*

The phase ends with the verification of all of the productions (dashed arrows in Figure 2.17). Coding verification concerns the control of the code's quality, mastering of complexity, compliance with methodological guidelines (naming rules, coding rules, tool chain constraints, etc.). All testing to be performed is described in the SVeP and results are formalized in the SRC-VR.

2.6.7. *Software integration testing*

2.6.7.1. *Objective*

In this step, we need to verify that the software architecture is correctly implemented in the software. To do this, we integrate the software part by part and verify that all interfaces are correctly connected. Integration testing is done by the integrator.

2.6.7.2. *Inputs*

– SVeP.

– Software/software integration test specification (S/S-ITS).

– Software/hardware integration test specification (S/H-ITS).

– Glossary (GL).

2.6.7.3. *Applicable procedures and guidelines*

– ITR plan type.

– ITR realization guide.

2.6.7.4. *Outputs*

– S/S-software integration tests report (S/S-ITR).

– S/H-software integration tests report (S/H-ITR).

– Anomaly (if it occurred).

– Integration verification report (INT-VR).

2.6.7.5. *Description*

Figure 2.18 shows the three activities that must be performed in this phase. From the code, we need to realize the components integration in order to obtain the final application. The process of software/software integration is defined in the S/S integration tests specification and we only need to implement it. As indicated in section 2.6.3, integration is done component by component. Note that the S/S integration does not require access to the target machine and can be performed on a development machine (host machine).

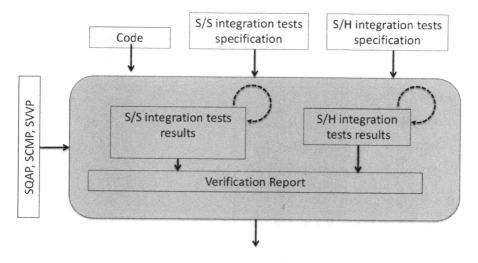

Figure 2.18. *Software integration process*

S/H integration can follow a specific strategy because there is a need for the target machine and some equipment to access information on the status of hardware components. The phase ends with the verification of all of the productions (dashed arrows in Figure 2.18). All testing that must be performed is described in SVeP and results are formalized in the INT-VR.

2.6.8. *Overall software testing*

2.6.8.1. *Objective*

The objective of this phase is to verify that the software that was produced conforms to its specification. To do this, we will perform the overall testing on the software application in its target environment.

2.6.8.2. *Inputs*

– SVaP.

– SVeP.

– Overall software validation test specification (OSTS).

– Project glossary (GL).

2.6.8.3. *Applicable procedures and guidelines*

– Overall software validation tests report (OSTR) plan type.

– OSTR writing guide.

2.6.8.4. *Outputs*

– OSTR.

– Anomaly (if it occurred).

– Software validation report (Sw-VAL).

2.6.8.5. *Description*

Figure 2.19 shows that the two activities in this phase are the realization of the overall testing of software on the target machine and the production of the validation report of software.

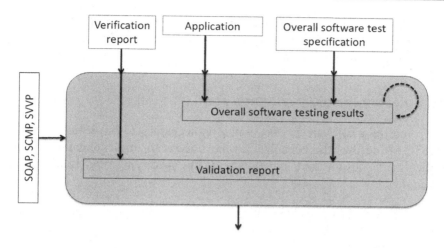

Figure 2.19. *Overall software testing process*

Overall software testing on the target machine demonstrates that the overall hardware and software verify the specification of software requirements on the final equipment.

The phase ends with the verification of all of the productions (dashed arrows in Figure 2.19). All testing that must be performed is described in the SVaP and results are formalized in the Sw-VAL.

2.7. Vocabulary and mode of expression

During all phases associated with the realization of a software application, it is necessary that the people involved interpret the documents in the same way.

To do this, it is necessary to define a unique vocabulary for the project through the establishment of a glossary (GL) and include modes of expression and descriptions that are understandable by all the people involved in the implementation of software application.

We must thus identify a glossary in the project documents and in the job procedures, a training that aims to define a common framework of expression and drafting of documents.

Verification procedures will help remove ambiguities and poor formulations. To do this, the associated checklists should identify rules to verify the understanding of texts.

2.8. Software quality assurance plan

To realize a software application, it is necessary to implement a SQAP. The SQAP defines the organization and means to implement the software application's design and development by specifying the role of each stakeholder.

The SQAP can be divided into several documents as we have shown in Figure 2.7. The SQAP must also describe the management of changes and non-conformities that may occur during the software's realization or operation.

Topics to be addressed are as follows:

– *Section 1*: refers to the identification of standards and mandatory regulations. The purpose of this section is to identify the set of standards and regulations to follow during the software's realization. It is necessary to identify the titles, references and versions of these documents. In this section, we find ISO 9001:2008, the CENELEC 50128:20xx standard, IEC 62279:20xx, DO 178:xx, CEI 61508:xxxx, etc.

– *Section 2*: includes project organization (software part), demonstration of independence and justification of competencies (it can rely on a local process and management of the company's human resources).

– *Section 3*: consists of a presentation of the scope of the software to achieve and identification of the software safety integrity level.

– *Section 4*: consists of a presentation of the quality control (metrics, checkpoints, audit, etc.).

– *Section 5*: includes presentation of the software realization cycle (V cycle, etc.) of each phase. For each one, a subsection should describe the input elements, output elements, activities to realize, human resources, technical resources (tools, testing environments, laboratories, etc.) and the criteria for the end stage acceptance and control.

– *Section 6*: includes a presentation of the configuration management (tool, procedure, version identification, identification of elements to manage, etc.). It will be necessary to explain how to produce the software version sheet.

– *Section 7*: deals with the presentation of the fault management process, requests for amendments and corrections.

– *Section 8*: deals with the presentation of the tool management process (identification, configuration management, etc.) and more particularly the management of tool qualification.

– *Section 9*: we must have a list of documents to be produced during the software's realization.

– *Section 10*: necessary to demonstrate compliance with the standards identified in Section 1, and more particularly with the CENELEC standard 50128 (or IEC 62279). Compliance with the CENELEC 50128 standard must not only be based on the tables at the end of Chapter 6 but on the whole standard. Indeed, the body of the standard is normative and some subjects are not treated through A.x tables. For example, in the 2001 version, testing coverage is not treated by an A.x table but by a phrase in the body of the document. For the 2011 version, the tool qualification is not treated by an A.x table.

2.9. Conclusion

This chapter represented an opportunity to present the development cycle in V cycle that allows for the realization of a software application and the activities to be performed have been introduced for all phases of this cycle.

The descending phase of the V cycle is fully detailed in Volume 3 [BOU 17a]. All verification techniques (testing, proofreading, static analysis, etc.) are presented in Volume 4 [BOU 17b].

Support Processes

3.1. Introduction

As presented in the first volume of this series [BOU 16], a software application's realization requires the definition of a strategy that is to be formalized in a software quality assurance plan.

This strategy should cover various aspects: the development method (see Chapter 1), verification and validation activities, personnel management, configuration management, tools management, etc.

Ultimately, this strategy is based on two types of processes: the so-called support process and the realization process. Figure 3.1 shows all the necessary processes for the realization of a software application. For each process, numbers are associated; they allow identifying the associated activities (see Tables 3.1–3.3).

This figure shows four types of processes:

– the processes related to the mastery of the customer's need and satisfaction. These two processes are consistent with the demands of the ISO 9001:2015 [ISO 15] standard (see Figure 9.1, Volume 1[BOU 16]);

– the processes related to the management of resources such as tools or competencies (5, 18 and 19);

– the processes related to the definition of a version, the software application's realization, a version's verification and delivery (see processes 2, 10–16, 9 and 17);

– the support processes that are existing and implemented processes for the software application's realization (1, 8, 4, 3, 6 and 7).

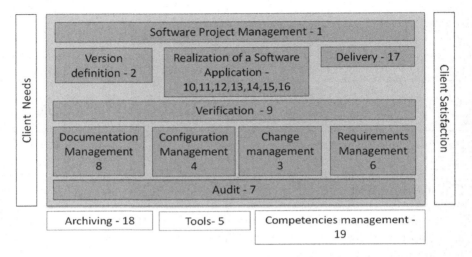

Figure 3.1. *Comprehensive view of a software application's realization process*

Id	Process	Description	Chapter or volume or section
1	Software project management	This process aims to manage the project in terms of cost, planning and resources.	S3.5
2	Version definition	The realization of a software application can be done through the production of several versions whose scope must be defined.	C6
3	Change management	Following the defects and/or evolution requests, it will be necessary to choose the changes to be made.	C6
4	Configuration management	The configuration of the software application in terms of files, documents, verification and tool trace to be formally defined and managed in time.	C7
5	Tool management	The implementation of the software application's realization process requires the use of tools that need to be bought, developed and managed.	C12 C13
6	Requirements management	The client's need is a set of requirements that must be demonstrated as assumed by the software application; a requirements management must be implemented	V1–C10

Table 3.1. *Description of the processes – part 1*

Id	Process	Description	Chapter or volume or section
7	Audit	The quality, configuration, subcontractor control, etc. through audits. The audits perform a spot check of the situation.	C15
8	Document management	The documentation associated with a certifiable software application is quite important. There are several reasons for this situation; we must ensure maintainability for an extended period, it must be shown that safety objectives are achieved, etc.	C7
9	Verification	Verification is an essential activity in the framework of realizing a certifiable software application. The objective is to demonstrate that the software application meets the client's need.	C9 V4
10	Specification	Based on the equipment, safety and knowledge of the hardware architecture requirements, a specification of software requirements is produced.	V3
11	Architecture	The software is divided into different components/modules. The components may be new, modified or reused.	V3
12	Design	For each component/module, the latter may be decomposed into a base element (function, procedure, class, etc.). Finally, the algorithms will be described.	V3
13	Coding	This stage consists of producing the code for a component/module.	V3
14	Component testing	For each stage of the descending phase (stages 10–13), it is necessary to show that the software application satisfies the need for which we will realize component/module, integration and comprehensive software application tests.	V4
15	Integration testing		
16	Overall software testing		
17	Delivery	At the end of the realization of a version of the software application, it will be necessary to make it available.	C6

Table 3.2. *Description of the processes – part 2*

Id	Process	Description	Chapter or volume or section
18	Archiving	At the end of the project, it is necessary to archive all the factors that enabled the software application's realization (tools, sources, methods, documentation, etc.).	C8
19	Competencies management	The project organization and competencies management are essential to a software application's realization having an impact on safety.	C4 C5

Table 3.3. *Description of the processes – part 3*

Figure 3.2 makes it possible to see a software application's realization cycle within a map of processes. Global processes such as the management of the client's needs, versions' definition, delivery, competencies management, archiving and management of customer satisfaction do not appear because they are global processes that are not dedicated to a given project, which we will now call the *transversal processes*.

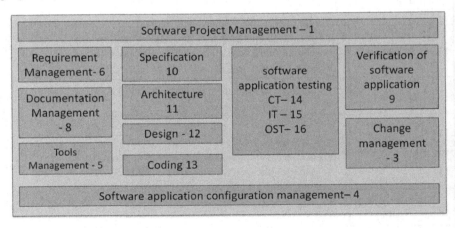

Figure 3.2. *Processes mapping related to a software application's realization*

3.2. Transversal processes

As we have previously indicated in the transversal process itself, we find:

– the client-related processes: client's need and satisfaction management;

– the processes related to the management of a version of the software application: definition versions, delivery and archiving;

– the processes related to resources management, such as competencies and tools management.

These processes are essential to the realization of a software application and/or a product and are not defined in the framework of the software application's realization process, but are used by this process. They must exist and be used.

3.3. Support processes

Support processes are necessary for the software application's realization and among them we find:

– *requirements management*: this process must cover all of the realization (from the client's need to the system to the software);

– *tools management*: special tools can be developed or purchased in order to carry out the software application. This process must include a tool qualification activity (see Chapter 13);

– *configuration and documentation management*: all software components (sources, testing scenarios, test results, analysis results, etc.), all the documents and all the tools should be managed in the configuration;

– *verification:* a process that applies to every stage of the realization cycle to ensure that no defects were introduced in the stage and that the product meets its needs;

– *change management*: this process is fundamental because the software application will evolve (defect correction, application development, porting the application, treatment of obsolescence, etc.).

Support processes are essential and can facilitate the software application's realization. They should be formalized and success depends on their stability over time. It is not possible to change methodologies with each project.

One of the principles of quality assurance lies in the fact that the methods and processes are *preestablished* and used *systematically*.

3.4. Principal processes

As part of Chapter 1, we discussed the fact that it is necessary to define a process for the software application's realization. This process follows a cycle that may be a V cycle, in cascade, in spiral, etc. There must be a cycle and it can be adapted to the software application's size and criticality. The principal processes were presented as part of Chapter 2.

3.5. Project management

Project management is an important support process. Indeed, it is necessary to manage the planning, costs and resources. The respect for the schedule may result in impacts on the software application's safety in the same way as the management of resources, especially human resources.

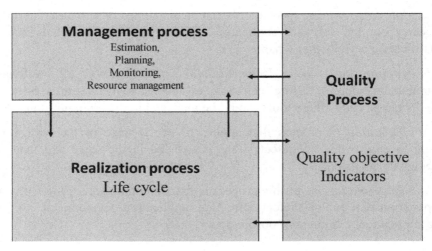

Figure 3.3. *Interaction between the processes*

Figure 3.3 shows the relationship between the production process, quality process and project management. Quality assurance must monitor the other two processes in order to ensure that the company's quality objectives are being met by the project. Project management aims to manage the resources available for the software application's realization process.

3.6. Conclusion

The software application's realization proceeds through the implementation of different process families:

– the principal processes that characterize the software application's realization; this is the heart of the business;

– the transversal processes that are implemented for products and software applications;

– the support processes are processes that allow the realization of the principal processes.

This processes approach is necessary and must allow us to better manage the software application's realization. Note that this approach allows us to build an applicable quality management system (QMS) that is especially accepted by the employees. Indeed, a QMS is only useful if it is deemed as facilitating a product's realization.

Organization

4.1. Introduction

As we have discussed in Chapter 9 of Volume 1 [BOU 16], the realization of a software application is performed through the establishment of an organization to cover the different needs that range from project management to safety demonstration through development and verification.

The establishment of an organization should help define reporting lines for a project, defining the connection to the services/departments of the company and ensuring independence when necessary. This organization must take into account the independence requirements that are inherent in certifiable applications.

Concerning the activities to implement, the first requirement concerns the project's quality control, which is done via the application of standards such as ISO 9001 and ISO 90003 for the software or via standards such as Capability Maturity Model for Integration (CMMI) or Software Process Improvement and Capability Determination (SPICE; [ISO 04]).

This chapter aims to present the requirements for the establishment of an organization.

4.2. Initial needs

The ISO 9001:2015 standard introduced the need for quality management, resource management, including human resources (competencies and training), and the need to manage product configuration. Concerning the development of a product, it is necessary to identify the responsibilities and groups of people that may be part of it.

In the context of applications that impact the safety of people (such as transportation systems and energy), it is necessary to set up a team responsible for managing reliability, availability, maintainability and safety (RAMS).

In order to better manage the human means, it is necessary to identify the types of activities that can be implemented as:

– quality management;

– realization of the software application;

– safety management.

This gives a fairly simple initial organization as shown in Figure 4.1. In this figure, the two support teams, quality and RAMS, are shown in gray.

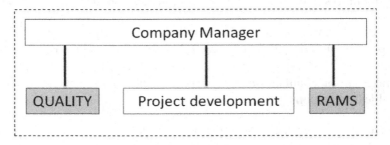

Figure 4.1. *Basic organization*

The realization of a software application is based on different families of activities, such as:

– the project management;

– the realization of the software application;

– the realization of verification and validation (V&V) activities;

– the management of the software application's configuration.

By taking this additional information into account, Figure 4.1 may also be shown as in Figure 4.2.

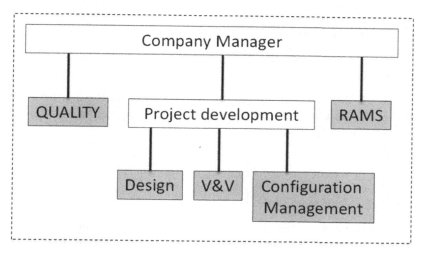

Figure 4.2. *Basic organization*

4.3. Realization of a software application

4.3.1. *Organization*

As stated above, to realize a software application, it is necessary to have different families of people with each family associated with a type of activity. Families are sometimes called roles and allow the characterization of responsibilities and competencies.

For a software application of safety, and as shown in Figure 4.1, the software project management team consists of:

– PM: the project manager is responsible for managing and organizing the activities of the realization of the software application;

– QUA: the quality engineer is responsible for verifying the implementation of quality procedures and corporate policies on the project and he/she should verify the correct implementation of the software quality assurance plan (SQAP), software verification and validation plan (SVVP), software configuration management plan (SCMP), and other relevant plans;

– SA: the person in charge of carrying out RAMS studies and in particular studies related to the software aspects (SEEA, CCR, follow-up of safety requirements, etc.).

Within the design team, there are three roles:

– RQM: the requirements manager, who is responsible for specifying requirements;

– DES: the designer, who is responsible for building the architecture and to realize the software design (component decomposition, predeveloped component reuse, algorithm descriptions, etc.);

– IMP: the implementer, who is charged to go from the design (description of algorithms and structural components) to an executable code.

Within the V&V team, there are four roles:

– INT: the integrator is responsible for carrying out the integration of software components that are already tested; this integration goes as far as obtaining the complete software. The integrator is also responsible for performing the software/equipment integrations tests;

– TST: the tester is the person in charge of performing the tests on a component or on the complete software;

– VER: the auditor is responsible for conducting audits, which may cover any document, file, process, etc;

– VAL: the validator is responsible for various activities to confirm that the software is considered validated or not.

Figure 4.3 give the complete organization for the realisation of a software application, and shows the following hierarchical relationships; the head of the QUALITY team is the hierarchical manager (solid line) of the person responsible for the quality of the project (same for the RAMS team). The PM has a hierarchical relationship (solid line) with the development team but the link is functional with the teams in charge of V&V.

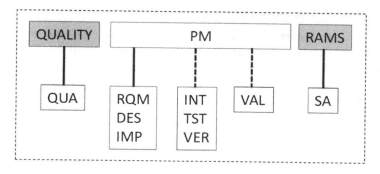

Figure 4.3. *Organization of a software project*

In the context of software applications that have an impact on people, it is generally recommended to evaluate the software's safety level and the compliance with applicable standards. The independent evaluation is carried out by a person external to the project. For greater independence, it is desirable that the person is external to the company. This person is appointed as an independent *evaluator* or *assessor* (ASR). Figure 4.4 shows that there are two independent organizations (dotted box).

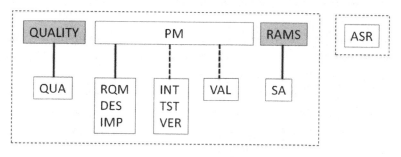

Figure 4.4. *Organization of a software project taking into account the independent evaluation*

4.3.2. Role

As we have already mentioned several times, it is necessary in the company to define roles (e.g. Table 4.1) in terms of responsibility and competency.

On this basis, it will be possible to define a process linked to the definition of an organization and another process related to the management of competencies. The management of competencies will be discussed in Chapter 3.

Role: Quality manager (QUA)
Responsibilities: – Should be responsible for the Software Quality Assurance Plan (SQAP).   – Should apply the company's quality assurance system in the project.   – Should define quality subjects in cooperation with the project manager.   – Should manage the quality assurance process of the software as defined in the SQAP.   – Should develop a software quality assurance report setting forth such quality assurance activities that have been planned in the SQAP.
Core competencies: – Should be competent in software quality management.   – Should understand and adapt the quality management in a given project.   – Should be competent in the software quality assurance activities in accordance with ISO 9001, ISO/IEC 90003, ISO/IEC 9126 standards.   – Should be competent in the company's quality system.   – Should be competent in software process improvement methods.   – Should have a comprehensive understanding of the software configuration management, control and traceability of documents, recording and analyzing data.   – Should be competent in performing audits.   – Should have a comprehensive understanding of software engineering.   – Should have a comprehensive understanding of project management.   – Should have an analytical thinking capacity and good observation skills.   – Should have good communication skills.   – Should understand the requirements of business standards.

Table 4.1. *The QUA role*

4.4. Conclusion

The realization of a product or a software application needs an organization to be put in place. This organization is based on the definition of hierarchical and functional relationships. In the framework that a software application has an impact on safety, it is necessary to introduce independence.

Functional links (see Figure 4.4 for the relationship between the PM and the VAL) will ensure that the PM can manage the project but will ensure independence. Independence can also be introduced by the hierarchical relationship as shown in Figure 4.4; the project QUA is independent of the PM.

The control of the organization and independence are important issues for software applications that have an impact on people's lives.

5

Human Resources and Competencies Management

5.1. Introduction

The quality control of a software application is not uniquely driven by the mastery of processes and control; it is necessary to have a group of competent, trained and experienced persons within the project in order to achieve the realization of a software application. As has been discussed throughout Volume 1 [BOU 16], the realization of a software application implements various processes in various fields and roles (project manager (PM), configuration management manager (CMM), validator (VAL), verifier (VER), etc.).

In Chapter 1, we had an opportunity to identify the necessary processes such as configuration management, quality control, project management, software development, verification, and testing. It is therefore necessary to first identify, based on the processes, the associated roles and job descriptions.

The general standards, such as ISO 9001 and business standards such as IEC 61508, introduce the need to control competencies. Clause 5 of CENELEC EN 50128:2011[1] [CEN 11] emphasizes the management of competencies and the formalization of this management.

---

1 In the 2001 version, CENELEC 50128 had already introduced the need to manage and demonstrate competencies.

A corresponding role is associated with one or more processes (see Tables 5.1 and 5.2). The job description (see Table 5.3 for example) aims to define the responsibilities associated with the role and the expected competencies for this role.

Process	Role	Competency
Project management	Project manager (PM)	Management Quality assurance Business standards
Safety management	Safety manager (SM)	RAMS
	Safety engineer (SE)	Configuration management Software Realization of a system Principles of verification and validation (V&V) Tools Business standards Applicable legal texts
Software realization	Requirements manager (RQM)	Requirement System Software RAMS Tools Business standards Applicable legal texts
	Software architect (SA)	Requirements Software architecture Software/hardware interface Business standards
	Designer (DES)	Requirement Component reuse Algorithms Language Business standards
	Implementer/coder (IMP)	Algorithm Language Programming Programming rules Compilation process Business standards

Table 5.1. *List of roles and associated competencies – part 1*

Process	Role		Competency
Quality management	Quality manager (QM)		Quality assurance ISO 9001:2015
Verification and Validation (V&V)	Verifier (VER)		Principles of V&V System Software/hardware interaction Software design Software architecture Language Programming rules Compilation process Verification technique Tools Business standards
	Integrator (INT)		Configuration management Software/hardware interaction Selection of test cases Test interfaces Software/hardware interface Tools Business standards
	Tester (TST)	Component tests	Configuration management Selection of test cases Host tests Tools Business standards
		Overall software tests	Configuration management Selection of test cases Tests on target Tools Business standards
	Validator (VAL)		Requirements System Software RAMS Business standards

Table 5.2. *List of roles and associated competencies – part 2*

It is then necessary to allocate human resources by giving them roles while verifying the suitability of individuals for the needs of the job description. A major difficulty lies in the fact that not all human resources are internal to the company and for budgetary reasons and/or expenses, it is necessary to use external resources and outsource certain activities related to the realization of the software application.

5.2. Definition of roles

Based on the list of processes, it is possible to identify the different roles needed to realize a software application (see Tables 5.1–5.3).

Process	Role	Competency
Configuration management	Configuration management manager (CMM)	Software configuration Management
Tool management	Tools manager (TM)	Tools Configuration management Tools qualification process Business standards

Table 5.3. *List of roles and associated competencies – part 3*

Tables 5.1–5.3 show the roles associated with the development of the software application (RQM, SA, DES and IMP), verification and validation (VER, INT, TST and VAL) and roles related to support processes (QM, SE, TM, CMM, etc.). For each role, it is necessary to define job descriptions outlining the responsibilities and skills.

Table 5.4 presents the role sheet associated with an RQM. Within the railway sector, the CENELEC EN 50128:2011 [CEN 11] and IEC 62279:2014 [IEC 14] standards in Appendix B of 62279 (which is normative) offer a job description sheet set (from which Table 5.4 is extracted), which may be completed.

Note that for each role, the need to know the standard (at least for the concerned part) and the regulatory framework is necessary.

Role: Requirements manager (RQM)
Responsibilities:
– Should be responsible for specifying the software requirements.
– Should be responsible for the software requirements specification.
– Should establish and maintain traceability to and from requirements of the system level.
– Should ensure that the requirements relative to specifications and software are included in change and configuration management, including the state, version, and the authorization status.
– Should ensure consistency and completeness in the software requirements specification (with reference to the user's requirements and the final application environment).
– Should develop and maintain the software requirement documents.
Main competencies:
– Should be proficient in requirements engineering.
– Should have experience in the field of application.
– Should have experience of safety criteria in the field of application.
– Should have quality management experience.
– Should understand the overall role of the system and the application environment.
– Should understand analytical techniques and their results.
– Should understand the applicable regulations.
– Should understand the requirements of the applicable business standards.

Table 5.4. *Sample job description sheet*

Table 5.3 may be formalized in the form of a sheet that combines the expected level and assessment for a given person (see Figure 5.1).

Competencies sheet: Requirements Manager

Competencies	Objectives Beginner = 1 Expert = 5	Actual level
Field: Railway signaling	5	4
Domain standards	5	4
Applicable regulation	5	3
Knowledge of Railway Systems	5	4
...		
Requirements management	5	5
Document writing	5	5

Figure 5.1. *Competencies of a requirements manager (RQM)*

Figure 5.2 introduces an example of a resources process that is organized around an allocation phase. As an input of the allocation phase, there are the job descriptions for each role defining the competencies and the expected level and the list of personnel, internal and external to the company, that must be involved in the project. As an output of the allocation, justifications that can show that the people allocated to each role are competent must be demonstrated. To do this, we must be able to link a person to a role and must have proof, which indicates that the expected competencies are assumed or if additional training is needed.

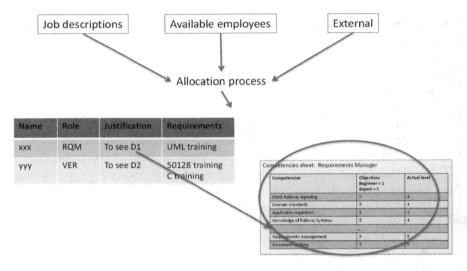

Figure 5.2. *Human resources allocation process*

5.3. Competencies management

Ideally, the software quality assurance plan must contain elements demonstrating the competence of persons depending on the roles that they assume, but this management may be formalized at the company's level.

In the context of software applications that have a safety objective, it is necessary to demonstrate that the people are competent with respect to the activities that they perform and toward the expected safety levels. Competencies management cannot be reduced to managing curriculum vitae

(CVs). Note that the management of CVs remains the most common minimum practice.

As previously introduced, we must have a process (see Figure 5.2), which, on the basis of participation in projects, identifies competencies and lack thereof (need for training or supervision during a future project).

Finally, we must actually implement a demonstration of the suitability of persons for a role. To do this, we must be able to assess the competencies of individuals, which requires formalizing their follow-up.

Name: Boulanger	Role							
	PM	QM	RQM	DES	IMP	VER	VAL	CMM
SIL 0	2	0	0	0	0	0	0	0
SIL 2	0	0	0	0	0	10	0	2
SIL 4	0	0	3	3	2	0	0	2

Figure 5.3. *Register of competencies by role*

The formalization of competencies has to go through the setting up of a register of competencies. This register is associated with an individual and used to store the activities already carried out (see Figure 5.3 that shows the time served in the role for each role and for each safety level), the competencies acquired (see Figure 5.4) or to be acquired and to evaluate the level. Compared to the CV, the competencies register is managed strictly by the company and reports information related to the assessment of the person.

Name: Boulanger	Technologies										Tools		...	...
	Meth-ods	Languages			Static analysis		Tests				Compiler			
	UML	SART	ADA	C	C++	Metrics	Progra mming rules	CT	IT S/S	IT H/S	OSTS	GNAT	GCC		
SIL 0	E	E	E	I	N	E	E	E	E	E	E	E	I		
SIL 2	E	E	E	I	N	E	E	E	E	E	E	E	I		
SIL 4	E	E	E	I	N	E	E	E	E	E	E	E	I		

E: Expert, I: Intermediate, N: Novice

Figure 5.4. *Competencies register by practice*

This competencies management should not only be applied to a company's personnel but also to the temporarily integrated providers' teams. For external persons, a similar but lightened process can be implemented (see Figure 5.5).

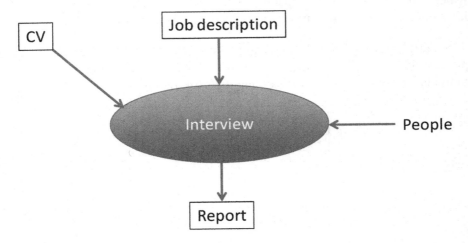

Figure 5.5. *Assessment of the competencies of an external person*

5.4. Outsourcing management

One of the challenges of competencies management is the competencies management of people external to the company (in-house, outsourcing, expert, etc.). The Labor Code and the laws of Commerce introduced a competencies management ban for external persons but ISO 9001:2015 does not allow external competencies management.

For in-house missions, Figure 5.5 shows a process of evaluation of the competencies of an external person. It is necessary to justify the adequacy of this process that is to be completed by an assessment over the various phases to ensure that the external person is adequate for his/her job. This assessment can be more regular in the beginning of mission and becomes annual as soon as the demonstration of competencies is achieved.

For outsourcing (package mission), it will be necessary to demonstrate that the contractor has a competencies management and an allocation management in place for the projects, and it will be necessary that the client makes at least one audit to check the suitability of this competencies management. In general, the audit of the subcontractor is performed simultaneously with the audit to demonstrate compliance to the ISO 9001:2015 standard.

In addition, for a safety-related project, it is important to ask for a justification of training to the industry standards – such as CENELEC EN 50128:2011 for the railway sector – and legislative environment.

5.5. Outsourcing

The outsourcing of activities requires the subcontractor to have a quality reference that is of the same level as that of the company. It is therefore necessary to set up a quality audit (ability to implement ISO 9001:2015 or a similar standard such as Capability Maturity Model for Integration and Software Process Improvement and Capability Determination) to verify that the referential exists and is actually implemented in the project.

5.6. Learning management

One of the problems of competencies management is linked to the competencies mastery of young recruits, persons undergoing changes, etc. It is therefore necessary to have a coaching or tutoring process, designed to accompany a person during the acquisition of a skill.

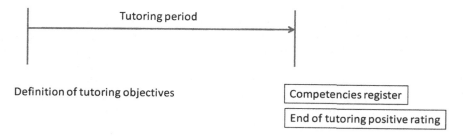

Figure 5.6. *Tutoring process*

The idea of the tutoring process (see Figure 5.6) is to define an evaluation process throughout various phases by a tutor. This tutoring has a start and an end date. Tutors may extend tutoring or confirm the acquisition of competencies.

5.7. Conclusion

The management of competencies is required to ensure the safety of the software application because it ensures that the persons involved will develop a preestablished and systematic process.

The management of competencies must take into account of all those involved in the project (internal, external, experts, interns, etc.).

Competencies management must evolve to move from a process based on a CV (which may be updated by the individual or by the commercial service) to a process based on a register of competencies that will be updated regularly by the persons involved in the project.

6

Management of a Software Application's Versions

6.1. Introduction

The realization of a software application is an activity that varies from very simple to very complicated. The level of difficulty depends on the size, the development time and the safety integrity level to be achieved. These parameters have an impact on the number of anomalies in the software application and on the number of detected and corrected anomalies. Hence, the need to upgrade the software application to reflect the correction of anomalies and/or change requests is necessary.

In addition to the correction of defects in the software application, it is also necessary to take into account new requirements and/or the evolution of initial requirements until the withdrawal of the system. Some changes may be imposed by the obsolescence of the equipment, components, equipment and/or supports software (operating system (OS), compiler, tools, etc.).

Finally, the changes are of three types:

– the increase in functionality;

– error correction;

– adaptation of a software application to a new context (hardware changes, support software changes, new interface, etc.).

In addition, time constraints may impact the implementation process and parallelize activities, production of intermediate versions, the implementation of the so-called *agile* approach, etc.

In Chapter 1, we identified three processes that are related to the management of a software application's versions:

– *definition of the version*: the goal of this process is to define a version's content. This process is applicable on an initial version and during a software application's maintenance phase;

– *change management*: it is necessary to define the processes related to the identification and treatment of anomalies and change requests, the decision process and the implementation of changes;

– *delivery of a version*: the goal is to define the process of delivering one version. We must therefore identify the tests to realize, required documents and delivery supports.

This chapter aims to present these three processes that are essential to the control of quality and safety.

6.2. Definition of the version

6.2.1. *Presentation of the need*

6.2.1.1. *Process*

During the launch of the realization of the first version of a software application or during a maintenance operation, it is necessary to define the scope of the version(s) that is (are) to be realized.

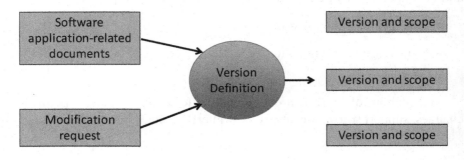

Figure 6.1. *Process of versions' definition*

To do this, we must implement a process called "definition of the version" (see Figure 6.1), which aims to identify the versions to be put in place and for each one to define the content of that version.

As part of the development of a complex application, it may be necessary to produce several versions and implement an iterative (see Figure 6.2) or incremental approach (see Figure 6.3).

6.2.1.2. Iterative approach

The iterative approach consists of implementing a realization cycle in which the activities are conducted in a predetermined sequence. This sequence shall be reproduced in the same manner as many times as necessary. This is what is meant by iterations. This realization cycle implies that the project is divided into a number of iterations. The duration of the iterations is not necessarily identical, in contrast to the so-called "agile" approaches for which the duration is fixed.

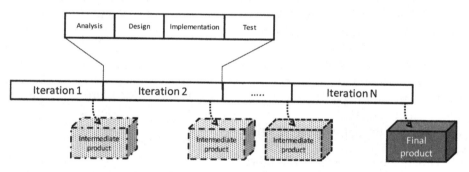

Figure 6.2. *Iterative approach*

The iterative approach is based on one of the following scenarios:

– either we know that the end user's needs are not fully known and, consequently, all of the requirements cannot be defined;

– or, all of the requirements are known but are taken into account only gradually (allowing an approach by risk analysis; see, for example, the spiral cycle [BOE 88]).

The iterative approach, based on the development of prototypes, allows the evaluation of concrete software elements. The first iterations are devoted to eliminating the major risks of the project and addressing the priority requirements and structuring for the continuation. It is during the first iterations that the architecture of the software application is defined. This architecture allows us to later on accommodate the iteration's production.

At each iteration, an intermediate version of the software application is made available. Iterations are not guided by the functionality to implement but by project objectives.

The iterative approach shows that at the beginning of each iteration, an *impact analysis* activity aims to identify the next version. This approach allows changes in direction in the light of what has been learned since the beginning of the project.

The latest iteration can be assimilated into a lifecycle in cascade by its activities and milestones. It formally validates consistency and completeness of all previous iterations' activities.

The overall software tests of the latest iteration can rely on the results of previous iterations. However, we must analyze the interdependencies between iterations and identify non-regression tests (for more information see Volume 4 [BOU 17b]) that must be passed in order to prove the correction of the software application.

This cycle of realization is more suited to projects of small or medium size. The product can potentially be delivered at the end of each iteration, but this is not an obligation.

6.2.1.3. *Incremental approach*

The incremental approach (see Figure 6.3) consists of successively realizing the functional elements of the product that are directly usable. The project is divided into a number of deliverable elements, which are called increments. Each increment is an operational product, partially in the beginning of the cycle (with a reduced perimeter) and totally in the end of the cycle (with a full perimeter).

An increment is a coherent functional part of the final product. It is characterized by the fact that:

– each increment adds new features;

– each increment is tested as a final product;

– the increments are defined in a prior way (which implies a prior classification of requirements).

The increments will be identified by taking into account various criteria as follows:

– essential functionality and/or accessories;

– technical and/or functional risks;

– provisioning timeline for system integration or client delivery.

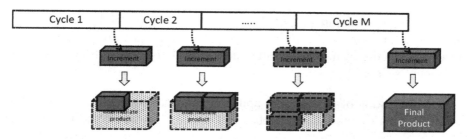

Figure 6.3. *Incremental approach*

The incremental approach is only possible if we have a clear idea of the software application's architecture and interfaces (we must not return to the parts that are developed at each increment) and the expected features are separable (ability to be developed independently). Like the iterative cycle, the duration of the cycles is not necessarily identical.

As shown in Figure 6.4, the incremental approach considers that a part of the software application has been defined in the first increment. The phases of specifications and architecture are realized in a unique manner in order to fix the features, performance, interfaces and safety principles, etc.

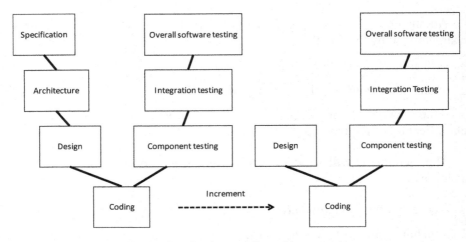

Figure 6.4. *Implementation of increments*

The implementation (detailed design and coding) and testing (unit, integration and overall) activities of software are split and conducted in successive steps, each of which incorporates and complements the previous increment's capacity.

The set testing of the software application's final increment can be based on the results of (partial) set tests conducted on the previous increments. However, for the result to be acceptable, we must analyze the interdependencies between these increments and include non-regression testing.

The number of increments is to be set early in the project or on the basis of a first architecture. For each increment, a goal must be set that will be linked to a set of function or set of requirement. Be careful not to set development increments of very short duration because excessive fragmentation of the development will effectively increase the cost of the process.

The implementation of an increment can be triggered in sequence or by feedforward. The cycle allows incremental recoveries between several increments or between successive operations. The recovery of increments allows the implementation of the development activities of the V_{N+1} increment when they are only slightly affected by the integration of the V_N increment. This is possible when the increments realize independent requirements or when the increments have little interaction.

An incremental approach necessarily involves the adoption, at least to some extent, of an iterative approach but the two concepts are not identical.

6.2.1.4. Implementation of specific versions

The need to produce multiple versions may be induced by the desire to establish an iterative/incremental approach but also by the need to allow the realization of specific actions such as tests (see Figure 6.5).

Figure 6.5 shows a "*roadmap*" approach that is similar to an iterative approach, but the versions' content is not defined by a functional but by a project need to carry out tests. More exactly, this approach begins iteratively but finishes with an incremental approach (the more complex the testing, the more it is necessary to have a version with a well-defined functional).

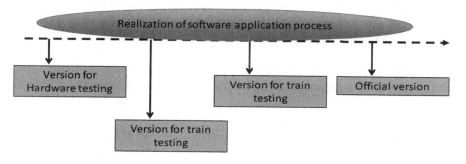

Figure 6.5. *"Roadmap" approach*

This discussion shows that project management cannot be summarized as a management of tasks, time and cost but good project management is based on anticipating needs and activities.

6.2.2. Implementation

The definition of version is an important process that aims to define the content of the new version to be produced on the basis of the existing version and the list of changes (change request and known anomalies).

As soon as the establishment of quality assurance (QA) and its formalization in the software quality assurance plan is completed, it is necessary to predict whether or not there will be the realization of several versions. It is quite difficult to postmodify the strategy without significant impacts on costs and/or time.

In very constrained fields such as the automotive, the establishment of a *roadmap* (see Figure 6.5) aiming to very quickly make versions available to testers is a necessity that allows one to meet very tight schedules (time-to-market).

6.3. Change management

6.3.1. *Presentation of the need*

During a software application's realization, verification activities will allow the detection and correction of anomalies. The project may decide to make available a version of the software application despite the existence of a certain number of anomalies. In addition, during the use of a software application, anomalies can be detected.

As shown in Figure 6.6, the change management process is divided into two activities: the creation of change requests and the processing of change requests.

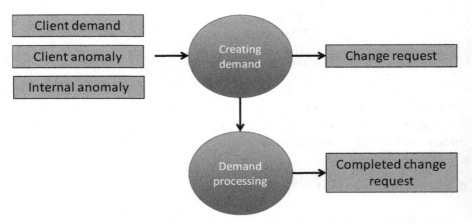

Figure 6.6. *Creation and processing*

As changes are inevitable in a project, it is essential to monitor any impact of these on the project. Change management is an important process that aims to manage change requests and anomalies from their identification to their conclusion. A change is a set of additions, modifications and deletions of data.

As shown in Figure 6.7, the processing cycle of a modification consists of several phases: identification, analysis of their effects (impact on safety and/or reliability of the software application), selection of anomalies to be corrected, analysis of anomalies, implementation and verification of corrections (in general, the verification of the proper implementation of the changes through a series of tests but it will be necessary to verify that no further changes have been implemented).

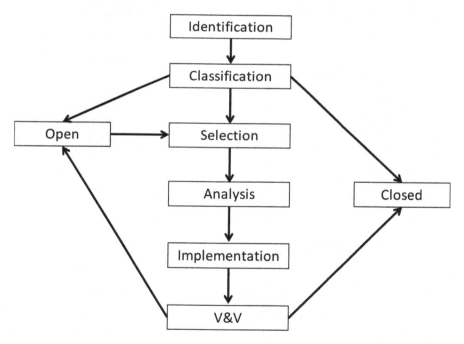

Figure 6.7. *Processing a change request*

6.3.2. *Processing of a change request*

6.3.2.1. *Presentation*

Change management is a process on the basis of the states of the defined demand in the context of Figure 6.7 that is divided into different phases as shown in Figure 6.8.

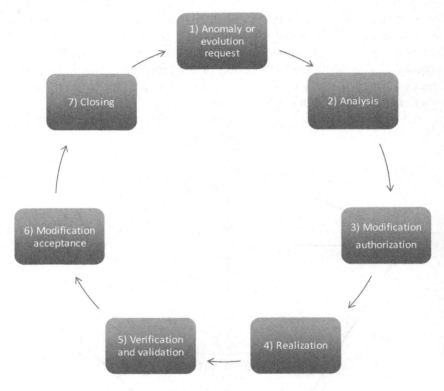

Figure 6.8. *Processing process of a change request*

The processing process of a change, as shown in Figure 6.8, is divided into several steps:

– *identification of the change*: in the context of this step, a client request or an anomaly has been identified;

– *change analysis*: on the basis of the change, we must analyze the impact of the latter on the whole software application in order to identify functional impacts, safety impacts, impacts on the verification and validation (V&V) activities and impacts on the costs and schedule;

– *authorize change*: the decision of whether or not applying a change is the result of a change management process, as shown in Figure 6.9;

– *realization of the change*: the change is carried out and the relevant documentation is produced;

– *V&V*: all V&V activities must be performed in order to verify that the change works properly;

– *acceptance of the change*: on the basis of previous activities, we must decide on the acceptance of the change. In case the V&V activities have shown that the change has not been properly carried out, a return to the previous phases will be necessary;

– *closing*: this step is to formally finalize the change if it was accepted.

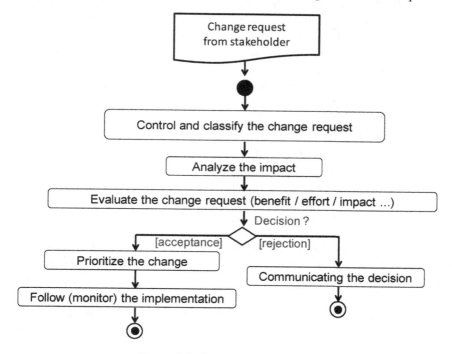

Figure 6.9. *Change management*

6.3.2.2. *Control and classification of the request*

The first stage of the change management process is to verify the compliance of the request and classify it. Does the request comply with the formality of a change request form if this file exists? Is all the information required for a first analysis present? If so, the committee in charge of managing the changes must be able to classify the request according to its degree of importance and emergency.

6.3.2.3. *Impact analysis*

When the first stage is carried out, the committee in charge of managing the changes will ask the operational teams of project to analyze the impact of the change request. This analysis must be carried out according to different points of view of the users and from static and dynamic (functional and non-functional) perspectives.

6.3.2.4. *Evaluate the change request*

In return for this impact analysis, the committee in charge of managing the changes must be able to assess in terms of cost, time and quality the possible scenarios for the realization and the impact on the project activities. On this basis, and in concert with the client, the committee in charge of managing the changes decides to make the change or reject the request. In the case of a rejection, there must be documentation and communication about the motives for the latter.

6.3.2.5. *Acceptance of the change request*

If the change request is accepted, the committee in charge of managing the changes prioritizes change activities in relation to ongoing work on the project and plans the delivery of change.

6.3.2.6. *Monitoring of the change request*

Regularly, during the change's realization phase, the committee in charge of managing the changes monitors the progress of activities related to the change. The change's implementation is not part of the committee's activities in charge of managing the changes. This realization is entrusted to an engineering project as per the normal processes (including elucidating, documenting, negotiating and validating the requirements).

6.3.3. *Impact analysis*

The analysis of anomalies is carried out through an impact analysis (definition 6.1) and non-regression analysis (definition 6.2).

The impact analysis aims to quantify (in cost, time and effort) the work to be done in each phase. This analysis helps to identify additions, deletions and changes to implement.

DEFINITION 6.1.– (IMPACT ANALYSIS). *The impact analysis of an anomaly consists of identifying the changes to be made on the descending phase (impact on the documents impact on the code, impact on the description and implementation of tests) of the realization.*

The non-regression testing aims to define the activities of V&V to be put in place to demonstrate that the change was properly carried out. In some cases, the non-regression is said to be total, and for this, it is necessary to re-execute all the verification (reviews, tests, etc.) of all phases. However, on the basis of impact analysis and non-regression, it is possible to identify the only necessary activities. In general, the non-regression consists of two parts: systematic verifications of activities that are dedicated to the change. The non-regression testing aims to minimize the cost of a new version.

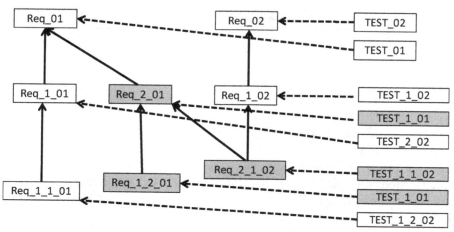

Figure 6.10. *Impact analysis*

DEFINITION 6.2.– (NON-REGRESSION TESTING). *Non-regression testing consists of determining a set of tests to prove that the change that was made has no effect on the rest of the software application[1].*

Requirements management is a tool allowing the control of changes. It is possible to define the impact cones associated with a modified requirement.

As shown in Figure 6.10, based on the changed requirements, it is possible to carry out the impact analysis. To do this, we extract the cone having as an origin the modified requirement going toward the code; this code allows the identification of all of the lower level requirements that are potentially impacted by the change and the cases of associated tests.

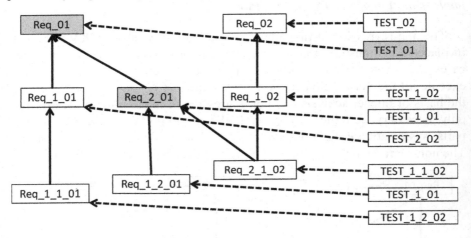

Figure 6.11. *Non-regression testing*

The second analysis (see Figure 6.11) consists of carrying out non-regression testing. Non-regression testing consists of building a cone that by the changed requirement goes back to the requirements of the input specification. On the basis of the cone of impacted requirements, we can thus select the non-regression testing to replay to show that the change has no impact on the system's need.

---

1 It should be noted that a non-regression test can be performed on software or on a more important element such as a device, a subsystem, and/or a system.

6.3.4. *Change control board*

In order to analyze change requests and to best control the influx of these requests, a Change Control Board (CCB) must be set up. This committee (called CCB) is a group of people responsible for making decisions to accept or reject the changes proposed by stakeholders.

The composition of a CCB will be based on the project type and the corporate sector. However, it is preferable that some stakeholders are systematically present in this organization. The typical composition of a CCB is given as follows:

– a change manager;

– a requirements manager;

– a configuration manager;

– a QA manager;

– a V&V manager;

– a safety assurance manager.

This list of people participating in the CCB is not exhaustive. It must be adapted to the context of the organization. The frequency of the CCB must be based on the project progress phase and on the amount and nature of change requests to process.

6.4. Delivery

6.4.1. *Presentation of the need*

Having arrived at the end of the software application's realization, it is necessary to provide a reference version of the software application; this version should be identified and formalized through a software version sheet (SVS). This activity is realized through the process that is called delivery (see Figure 6.12).

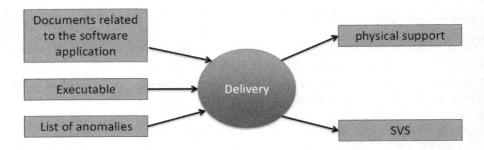

Figure 6.12. *Production of the SVS*

The SVS should uniquely identify the software application. Also, the software application's reference and version are not sufficient and it is necessary to provide means (verification of a checksum for example) to verify the software application's integrity. This verification is necessary because this software application will be delivered through a physical medium (USB, CD, DVD, etc.) and will be transferred to the final system via a download tool.

6.4.2. *Implementation*

The production of the SVS is done through the analysis:

– of the version's perimeter;

– of the configuration (software, documents, tools, etc.);

– of the residual faults;

– of the exemptions related to the non-application of the process.

The SVS must identify:

– the compatibility between the software and hardware;

– the compatibility between the produced software and the other software (such as OS version, maintenance tool version, etc.);

– the version of the executable, version of the sources, the version of applicable documents;

– the identification of the software elements needed to verify that the software is the one that should be installed;

– the limitations of use.

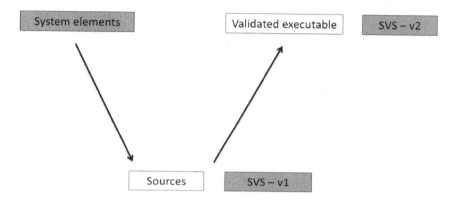

Figure 6.13. *V cycle and two versions of the SVS*

In view of the V cycle that is conventionally used (see Figure 6.13), it is necessary to produce at least two versions of the SVS. A first version of the SVS must be published at the end of the descending phase in order to make a version of the software application available to perform the V&V activities. The first version will allow the setting of the version of the sources in configuration and the V&V activities can clearly identify the analyzed elements. The second version will be produced at the end of the ascending phase.

Note that the CENELEC EN 50128:2011 standard [CEN 11] identifies specific needs that must be taken into account by the SVS in order to achieve the deployment of the new version. Among the requirements, we find the need to identify the compatibility between the software application and other software and with the different hardware.

6.5. Conclusion

This chapter was an opportunity to present the three activities (definition, change management and delivery) related to the management of a version. It is essential to understand and master these three activities well because they determine the work method. Indeed, it is not possible to imagine managing a single version at the end of a project, as it is not possible to imagine having no fault in a software application. The SVS is essential for managing the software application (knowledge of the perimeter, identification of limits, etc.), including the deployment of a new version. The management of a version will support the concept of configuration management that will be treated in Chapter 7.

6.6. Appendix A: change request

A change request is composed of three parts. The first part contains the following elements:

– identification of the reference version on which it is desired to apply a change;

– identification of the initiator: internal client, external client;

– identification of the type of change: improvement, new functionality, fault correction, etc.;

– description of the change;

– identification of planning constraints;

– the name of the person in charge of carrying out the analysis of changes;

– the potential impact on safety: it will be asked of the safety team to give an opinion on the impact of this on the overall safety.

The second part is to be drafted by the person who realized the change analysis. It must contain the following elements:

– the identification of changes to be realized;

– the identification of the impacts of the change (list of changes for each level);

– the identification of the V&V strategy of the change (identification of activities to be performed, delta tests, partial or complete validation, etc.);

– non-regression testing: list of tests to be carried to the next level to show that the change does not change the overall behavior;

– list of changes to postpone to the next level: system adjustments may be necessary, for example the addition of a software interface requires adapting the system;

– the name of the person implementing the change (realization and V&V);

– list of potential incompatibilities to manage: incompatibility between the software application's version application with other software or hardware (OS and driver included).

The third part is to be drafted by the person who was in charge of implementing the change. It must contain the following elements:

– the identification of the version containing the change;

– the identification of changes that were made: lists of documents, files and tools;

– the verification that the changes made are consistent with what has been provided in part 2;

– the results of the V&V activities;

– the verification that the realized V&V activities are consistent with what has been provided in part 2;

– the list of faults that were identified during the implementation of the V&V activities;

– limits and constraints of use.

6.7. Appendix B: SwVS

An SwVS consists of the following elements:

– identification of the software application: name, reference and version;

– identification of the configuration associated with this version: a configuration can be based on several tools located in different places and may be characterized by a specific tag, etc.;

– identification of the version's contents:

  - list of documents and associated versions,

  - list of source files and associated versions,

  - list of result files and associated versions,

  - list of tools with their references and associated version;

– identification of the limits and constraints of uses;

– identification of known faults;

– identification of the executable generation process;

– identification of software applications in interface (other software, maintenance software, etc.) and compatible versions;

– identification of compatible hardware platforms;

– identification of hardware in interface (measuring tool, maintenance pc, etc.) and compatible versions.

7

Configuration Management

7.1. Introduction

Configuration management (CM) [ISO 03] consists of controlling changes in the system over time. The realization of a system requires managing the various parts and their changes. For a software application, the situation is even more complex because of the presence of source files, tools or documents whose changes need to be controlled. CM is implemented in order to control complex systems in all fields: information technology, aerospace, automotive, railway, aeronautic, nuclear, space systems, defense, etc.

CM is a major process in numerous standards associated with quality control such as ISO 9001:2015 [ISO 15], ISO/SPICE [ISO 04] and Capability Maturity Model for Integration[1].

CM of a software application is a discipline supporting project management that allows the definition, identification, management and control of configuration items (CIs) throughout a software application's realization cycle.

As a general rule, a CI is a set of hardware, services or a subset defined thereof, selected for CM and processed as a single entity in the CM process.

---

1 See the website of CMMI Institute: http://cmmiinstitute.com/.

As already mentioned, for a software application, a CI is one of the elements necessary for the production of this software application:

– documents;

– files related to models, sources, etc.;

– commercial off the shelf (COTS);

– library;

– files related to verifications, tests, analyses, etc.

– tools developed within the project's framework;

– tools of the trade used within the project's framework.

7.2. Configuration management

7.2.1. *Principles*

CM may be used for several purposes:

– to store and track the different versions or revisions of any information intended to be used by a system (hardware, software, document, requirement, unit data, etc.), which is the main use;

– to deploy a system's or software's configurations and/or restore old configurations ("roll-back").

In CM, there are four main activities:

– identifying the CIs: documents, requirements, other artifacts;

– saving the configuration states: by saving all the successive states (versions) of a configuration article and the configuration itself;

– controlling the configuration: by maintaining consistency of all the configuration data for the entire system's lifetime (in relation with the change in management);

– auditing (see Chapter 15) the configuration: to do this, we realize reviews and/or verifications of the configuration repository's integrity.

CM is closely linked to version management (see Figure 7.1) and meets some principles of the latter:

– trunk: it is involved in the development of main trunk (main branch);

– branch (or checkout): application of a divergent change (new branch) from the main trunk of development and which occurs without conflict (which is done voluntarily and with the agreement of project's different stakeholders);

- merge (or commit): application of a branch's fusion with the development's main trunk,

- tag: reference version corresponding to a level of maturity of the development.

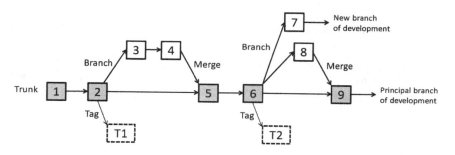

Figure 7.1. *Version management*

7.2.2. *Formalization*

CM is one of the pillars of the success of a software project and it is necessary to have a strong, equipped and controlled process. CM must therefore rely on:

– a methodology that is described, known and applied;

– proven and adequate tools;

– competencies, in general we appoint a configuration manager (see Table 7.1).

At the project level, all configuration management aspects must be formalized in a configuration management plan (CMP). At the software level, we need to manage some documents, many files (sources file, test files, analysis result, etc.), many tools (compiler, editor, etc.) and some equipement (computer, test bench, etc.). This is why we introduce a software configuration management plan (SCMP).

7.3. Software application CM

7.3.1. *Introduction*

A software product is the association of the software application in a particular configuration. A software application is managed independently in configuration and is considered a by-product. Each software application consists of components or software functions managed independently from one another, which are called constituents. Each constituent is managed independently in configuration.

In software engineering, branches are generally created for the purpose of anomaly corrections and software maintenance. When the software application is stable, we proceed to *merge* changes made on the secondary branch to the main branch. The branches can be used to realize a version dedicated to a specific use.

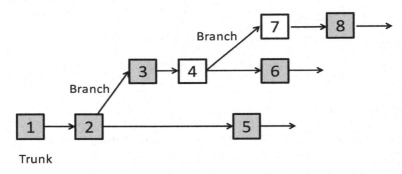

Figure 7.2. *Branches*

In certain cases (Figure 7.2), in the development of a family of products for example, a new development branch is created introducing greater independence and a rupture in the development chain (Figure 7.2 – configurations 3 and 7).

The introduction of branches introduces two difficulties that have an impact on the implementation and maintenance costs:

– it becomes necessary to manage compatibilities and incompatibilities between versions within the same system or during the communication between systems;

– it becomes necessary to introduce a process that allows managing faults detected on a branch to report these to another branch if necessary.

The management of versions of an application is theoretically simple but is not in practice. Therefore, it is necessary to implement, from the project's beginning, good practices to allow the coexistence of all the version lines and tools for the management process.

7.3.2. *Software component's configuration*

As shown in Figure 7.3, in a software component's configuration, we must find the following elements:

– documents;

– files related to models, sources, etc.;

– library;

– COTS;

– files related to verifications, tests, analyses, etc.;

– tools developed within the project's framework;

– tools of the trade used within the project's framework.

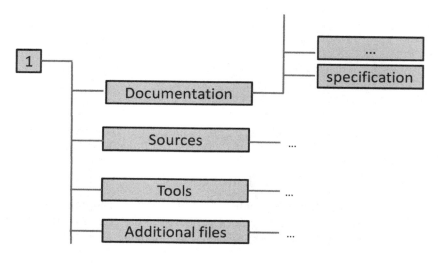

Figure 7.3. *Component configuration*

7.3.3. *Product line*

Figure 7.4 shows the process of a software application's realization based on the concept of a product line. The generic product is not a complete application, it is necessary to implement a specialization stage that allows defining the common boundary between the trunk and the generic application to be realized; from thereon, it is possible to build the generic application on a common base.

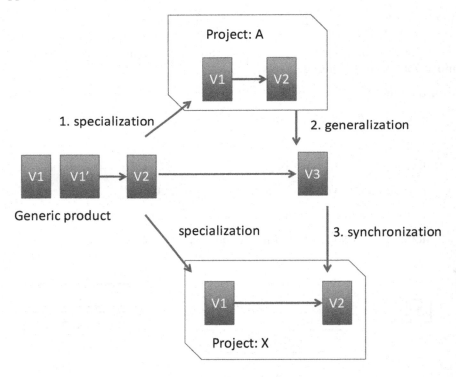

Figure 7.4. *Product line*

This process is associated with two activities:

– the first one, called the generalization, allows bringing the generic application's behaviors that have been validated to the common trunk so that we can use them in a subsequent software development;

– the second activity is called synchronization and is related to bringing a generic application back to a level in relation to the common trunk; indeed, the common trunk may have evolved (fault correction, generalization, etc.).

7.3.4. *Preexisting components*

Preexisting components are of two kinds:

– the COTS, which are purchased components that are provided as such with a minimum of documentation;

– reused components, which are software applications, libraries or components realized during previous developments. Thus, they already have a history and experience feedback. We therefore seek to use them without changing them.

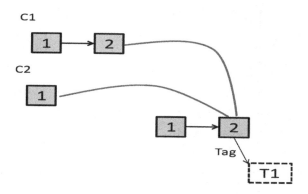

Figure 7.5. *Use of preexisting components*

In both cases, it is necessary to manage these preexisting components in configuration (Figure 7.5), but this management is to be realized at the company level and not at the project level. A CM plan aims to manage the relation between the components.

7.3.5. *Generic software and instantiated software*

As has already been mentioned several times, software applications are generally parameterized (see Figure 7.6) in order to introduce the ability to change the behavior with a minor modification (a parameter change).

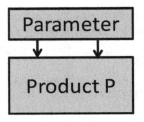

Figure 7.6. *Parameterized product*

It is therefore necessary to manage two levels of configuration, a product configuration (generic product, parameter, etc.) and a final product configuration.

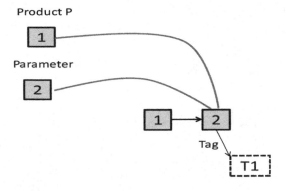

Figure 7.7. *Two levels of configuration*

As shown in Figure 7.7, the configuration of an instantiated version of the product is a combination. Note that, finally, we have 2 levels of configuration, indeed, and to this the configuration of hardware and other software applications must be added.

7.4. Implementation

The software is part of the equipment that must be managed in configuration; this is why a "configuration management plan" is necessary. The CMP must cover all of the equipment's aspects: pneumatic, mechanical, electrical, electronic, *hardware*, software, maintenance tools, etc. The CMP describes the naming rules, version management rules, CM means, organization, responsibilities, etc., and the content of the version sheet.

Concerning the software's CM, the list of elements produced in the context of the software application's realization and the associated versions must be known at all times.

Sources and the executable's generation process are only a few elements of the software's realization and all the documents produced should not be omitted (plans, specification, design documents, test records verification documents, end of phase report, etc.), different scenarios and test results[2] (CT, S/S IT and S/H IT OST), tooled verification phases results (coverage summary file, metrics summary file, code analyzer report, etc.) and the tools being implemented throughout the process.

Role: Configuration management manager (CMM)
Responsibilities:
– Must be the manager of the configuration management system.
– Must ensure that all software requirements are clearly identified and implemented in versions independently within the configuration management system.
– Must prepare delivery sheets that mention the incompatible versions of software components.
Core competencies:
– Must be proficient in software configuration management.
– Must understand the IEC 62279 requirements.

Table 7.1. *Extract from table B.10 of the IEC 62279:2014 standard*

The control of the software CM goes through the implementation of an SCMP. The SCMP is designed to define the general approach (what, when and how), the tree(s) to archive all of the elements (sources, documents, files, tools, etc.) and the persons in charge of managing and controlling the CM. The proposed process should define the content of the software version sheet. The IEC 62279:2014 standard introduces a specific role for this activity and a sheet (Table B.10 of IEC 62279).

---

2 Unit testing strategies (UT), component testing (CT), integration testing (IT) and overall software testing (OST) will be presented in Volume 4 of this series [BOU 17b].

The CMP must identify a control activity; it is not acceptable to discover at the end of the project that elements are lost or that the configuration is incoherent. This verification activity can be done through configuration audits. These audits (see Chapter 15) can be realized by the quality team.

7.5. Conclusion

This chapter has been an opportunity to demonstrate the importance of CM for a product as well as for a software application. We have shown that it is not a CM per say but that there were several levels of configuration and it is necessary to manage the consistency and compatibilities between configurations.

CM guarantees the control of a version and also helps ensure long-term maintainability and reusability. Reusability is essential for the control of costs and efforts. The maintainability of a critical and safe operational system is in general a need that goes from 15 to more than 40 years.

8

Archiving

8.1. Introduction

After delivering a version of the software application, and without the need to maintain it, all of the project's elements should be archived.

The life expectancy of applications, having an impact on safety, ranges from 15 to 50 years (see the discussion on the proposal to change the lifetime of nuclear plants to 80 years).

This archiving of applications that have an impact on the safety and/or are certified is also linked to legal constraints; in case of an incident or accident, the application is needed to be able (upon request) to replay a certain activity.

Thus, archiving is designed to ensure the option of reinstalling the project and the related means in order to generate the executable, replay activities (such as tests) and to be able to produce a new version of the software application.

The generation of the executable may be necessary in the event of loss, obsolescence (operating system (OS), processor, etc.) or in case of an incident (regulatory request, etc.).

8.2. Archiving process

8.2.1. *Principle*

Figure 8.1 presents the archiving process. As an input, we have all of the software project's elements (documents, tools, source file, test results, etc.) and all must be consistent with the software version sheet (SVS). Therefore, there is a verification stage of the configuration to be carried out in order to ensure that nothing is missing.

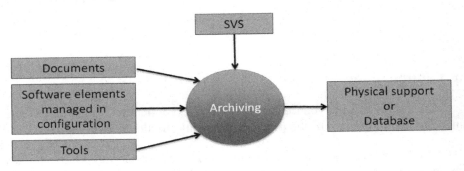

Figure 8.1. *Archiving process*

Once all of the available elements are verified, it is possible to create an archive. This archive must be robust and we must set an archiving duration (5, 10, 15 years, etc.). The archiving duration is dependent on the contract, context and risks.

Depending on the duration, the archiving media and/or process must be adapted. The archiving on an external drive requires the implementation of a verification process and a regular change in disks.

8.2.2. *Archiving of sources and other products related to the software application*

On the basis of the SVS, it is possible to identify the space containing the source files, test files (scenarios, result files, coverage files, etc.) and files related to code analyses such as the verification of metrics and the verification of programming rules. The archiving of source and annex files is simple and poses no problem (in the worst-case scenario, we produce a copy of the configuration management or a compressed file of the whole).

In fact, there exists a difficulty related to the management of preexisting software and Commercial Off The Shelf (COTS). For preexisting software, it is necessary to restore some elements to the configuration that were perhaps not already restored.

For the COTS software, the situation is more complicated as it could be concerning a software component, which was purchased from another party or that was recovered. In both cases, the documentation and annex files (tests, analysis, etc.) are limited or non-existent.

In the category of COTS, we find so-called "free" software, such as eCOS[1] for example. The particularity of these so-called "free" COTS is that the only accessible documentation is a website that can disappear at any time. Access to the source files is not a guarantee of quality and/or capacity to maintain but it allows the expectation to develop a new version. In general, documentations are in HTML and are not so easy to copy and manage locally.

8.2.3. *Tool archiving*

Initially, purchasing a product gives rise to a distribution medium and a license. The distribution support has evolved from the simple floppy disk to a DVD containing an entire environment and documentation. The license could be associated with a machine or a company. In this context, tool archiving goes through the locking of the distribution support of licenses and, in some cases, machines allowing the completion.

A first change occurred with the notion of the testing license (one of the examples concerns the Field Programmable Gate Arrays programming related tools), as well as certain testing license projects (renewed several times) that were used, posing a problem for the identical regeneration of the executable.

---

1 To learn more about eCOS, see the website at: http://ecos.sourceware.org.

The second change occurred with the advent of dematerialization, where the purchase of software no longer comes with installation support and a license, and the file is retrieved directly from the web or installed on a server along with the use of license outside the company. This poses a problem for the development of archiving and its control in time.

8.2.4. Machine archiving

Having a tool archive (supports and license) is not a guarantee of the ability to identically regenerate the executable and/or to be able to replay the previously implemented activities. Indeed, the tools may be dependent on the executing machine, on an OS and third-party tools (such as drivers, utilities, etc.).

Initially, the solution was to archive already used machines and new machines. With older technologies, this type of approach could work despite problems related to storage.

With new technologies, many defects appear on the stored elements. However, the difficulty remains with the OS and third-party software as it is not easy to reinstall all software identically on a new machine.

In some fields, such as the automotive industry, the concept of iso-functionality was introduced to manage the various problems linked to the tool versions, machine characteristics, OS versions and third-party software versions. This notion of iso-functionality is interesting but not always acceptable; indeed, in the field of critical applications, a necessity to be able to identically replay certain activities is present.

To conclude this section, it should be noted that the implementation of a virtual machine that is a copy of an existing machine is the solution that is mostly developed, as it can be free from the OS version and third-party software.

8.2.5. Document archiving

In order to maintain software applications, the documentation of projects should be archived.

Documentation archiving is not simple because we must guarantee the option to access and edit the documents. Opening a document with a new version of a tool is not guaranteed (because of ascending compatibility); this is the reason why it is advisable to archive the document in its native format and in a format such as PDF.

Initially, the complementary version was a paper version, but paper is subject to multiple disadvantages, such as storage and destruction (due to pests, humidity, etc.).

A PDF version will perhaps not allow for easy modification but ensures the ability to read and edit the document in a few years time.

8.3. Conclusion

Software application archiving concerns several elements: sources, documents, tools and machines. This need for archiving shall be taken into account before the completion of a project.

Quality control standards as well as business standards do not identify any specific process or activity. Therefore, the necessary steps are taken voluntarily.

Maintenance of a Software Application

9.1. Introduction

One of the difficulties associated with software applications is their maintenance throughout the system's lifespan. Critical systems such as transport, energy and/or defence systems have as a main feature "a long lifespan". This lifespan ranges from 15 to 40 years. It should be noted that following recent discussions related to nuclear power plants, we are now looking at 80 or even 100 years (see last EDF request).

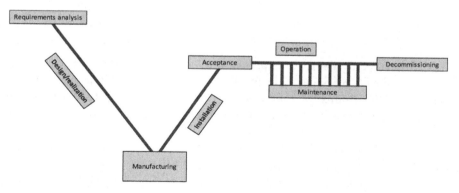

Figure 9.1. *Cycle taking maintenance into account*

Software faults introduce another difficulty; at the core of all software applications, there are some known faults and some which are yet to be discovered. One of the significant changes is the fact that a few years ago we put systems with a low rate of residual bugs into service, but in view of the size of the latest software applications, the very short realization deadlines and the large amount of applications, software applications with a more important rate of residual bugs were put into service with the need to correct a large number of these during the guarantee phase (which ranges from 1 to 2 years).

Faced with this change, it is necessary to have an application maintenance process that aims to control the evolution of the software while ensuring the level of quality and safety.

Business and quality standards (such as ISO 9001 [ISO 15]) introduce maintenance only partially; in general, they focus on change management and associated analyses (impact analyses and non-regression). The CENELEC EN 50128:2011 (and IEC 62279 [IEC 14]) standard formalizes the context of software changes by linking them to the system's changes (see the link with phase 13 of the CENELEC EN 50126 [CEN 00] standard) and makes a link with the need for deployment. The maintenance of a software application is described in section 9.2 of the CENELEC EN 50128:2011 standard. IEC 61508 and ISO 26262 also introduced some requests for system and software maintenance.

9.2. Principles

Maintenance of a software application is a real challenge. Indeed, it does not only consist of being able to change the code, but it is necessary to guarantee a continuity of the services provided by a software application during a more or less long duration and on equipment that may be different.

The difficulty is not about managing the software but rather handling requests from multiple clients using the same software in different versions. The deployment registry identified in Chapter 10 thus becomes very useful. When a new version is decided, time should be taken to verify if the change request or fault correction is compatible with all deployed versions or if there is the risk of creating a branch introducing incompatibilities. This decision must be reasonable as it can have important financial impacts on the project.

In Chapter 6, we discussed the change in the management SMP process, and now we need to describe the realization process of a new version that implements a lot of changes. This process rests on the fact that the previous version is in service and meets quality and safety objectives. It is therefore necessary that the new version complies with the same objectives.

The maintenance of a software application may be implemented to take two types of changes into account:

– the correction of a software fault;

– taking a change request into account:

  - adding functionality,

  - adding messages according to new system features,

  - an adaptation or change in implementation following component obsolescence.

The correction of a fault does not change the overall behavior of the software application and the impacts on the encompassing system are limited. Taking into account an evolution request seeks to add (adding features, adding messages, etc.) or withdraw (withdrawal of a feature, etc.) behaviors that have an effect on the encompassing system.

The modification of a software application can have impacts on the software/software and software/hardware compatibility. Also, compatibility is a point that needs to be verified.

On the other hand, evolving the software application can impact the system, and adaptations of the latter may be necessary.

9.3. Realization of the new version

9.3.1. *Process*

It is necessary to have a software maintenance plan (SMP). This SMP should describe the realization process of a new version on the basis of a given version and a set of evolutions. Figure 9.2 shows the maintenance process in four phases. Table 9.1 describes each phase precisely.

The maintenance activity's output is a new version of the software application that is characterized by a software version sheet (SVS).

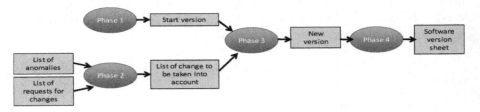

Figure 9.2. *New version*

Id	Title	Activity description
1	Identification	The objective of this phase is to identify the software application's initial version that will be submitted to the maintenance process.
2	Selection of evolutions	If there is a new version, it is necessary to identify the changes to be taken into account (subsets of anomalies and/or subset of the client's evolution demands) (see Chapter 6)
3	Realization	This activity consists of realizing the new version (development, tests and verification).
4	Delivery	Once the software application's version is validated, the whole must be put in configuration and must be delivered. To do this, we must produce a SVS.

Table 9.1. *Maintenance process tasks*

9.3.2. *Constraints related to maintenance and deployment*

9.3.2.1. *Protection of the executable*

The executable must be protected (checksum, MD5, etc.) so that we can verify that during the transportation and various downloads the version has not been altered.

9.3.2.2. *Static versus dynamic*

Initially, software applications were delivered in the form of an executable that is said to be static. That is, all of the libraries were part of the executable.

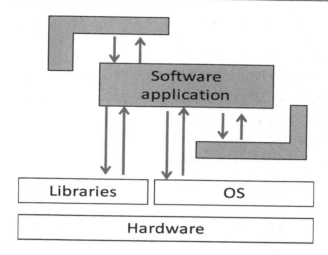

Figure 9.3. *Dynamic executable*

Now, it is nearly impossible to produce a static executable, and we are left with a dynamic executable (an executable accompanied by its libraries). This dynamic executable may also use the libraries available within the operating system.

The deployment of a dynamic executable's new version on a previous version can lead to a situation where the final installation is a mixture of the two versions. This situation can also occur in the case of incremental deployment (different versions can be made up of a set of different files). This can occur if files are being read or in the case of manual installation. If there is a protection for the dynamic executable, it will not allow the detection of a mixed installation.

9.3.2.3. *Identification of the executable*

Once the installation is realized, it is necessary to be able to identify the installed version; in order to do this the software application must be able to provide an identifier. This identifier can be displayed on the screen or on another medium (such as through LEDs on the equipment's front panel) and/or sent to the output related to the maintenance.

9.3.3. *The software version sheet*

The SVS is a document that is essential for software application management and control. The SVS is a document that must identify:

– the input version of the maintenance process;

– the list of changes taken into account (fixed anomalies and/or change requests taken into account);

– the characterization of the version;

- list of the project's documents (complete list or list of modified documents),

- list of source files and version,

- identification of x,y,z version (see configuration management),

- protection of the executable;

– the list of known anomalies;

– the list of usage restrictions (non-implanted functions, bound, etc.).

9.4. Conclusion

The maintenance of a software application is an element that is essential for ensuring the system's functioning. It is necessary to write an SMP at the end of the project, which will outline the guidelines for maintenance.

Maintenance uses the concepts that have been identified in Chapter 6 concerning the control of versions but it is also an input for the deployment phase, which is described in Chapter 10.

Deployment of a Software Application

10.1. Introduction

As already mentioned, critical applications have a longer life expectancy and an obligation in terms of availability that may be strong, such as for transport and energy production.

This is why, in the case of development of software applications, a deployment process of new versions is needed to ensure that the installation will be controlled and would, at worst, be able to return to the previous state. The deployment of a software application's version is a process that must accompany the maintenance activity.

10.2. Principles

The business standards such as the IEC 61508, ISO 26262, the CENELEC EN 50126 [CEN 00] standard, etc., recommend the control of the system's safety, not just during the realization (from design to manufacturing) but until the withdrawal of the system. The impact is that it is necessary to control developments and demonstrate that the level of safety integrity is the same after the modification of one or more parts of the system.

This request has several impacts on the process:

– it is necessary to integrate the maintenance capabilities within the system during the design stage;

– it is necessary to define the maintenance processes during the realization phase and they should be evaluated by an independent evaluator;

– any modification must be identified and authorized;

– the modification process of a system in service must follow the maintenance plans;

– the deployment of a version must be planned and authorized;

– following a deployment, the new configuration must be registered and the operating procedures must take into account the new exported constraints if they exist; please note that there may be constraints from the previous version that need to be removed.

It is worth noting that the software deployment's management is recommended by the 2011 version of the CENELEC EN 50128 standard within its section 9.1. With its IEC (IEC 62279) version, these are the only domain standards that clearly identify this process at the level of the software application.

10.3. Implementation

The availability of a software version is done through provision of a software version sheet (SVS) that shall identify:

– the software's version;

– the software's configuration (list of relevant documents, list of sources, elements of configuration management, etc.);

– user constraints;

– limitation (some functions are not available or we need to limit the speed);

– the elements characterizing the interface elements: the hardware version, the operating system version, software version, the software interfaces version, etc.

The deployment of the software is linked to replacing an existing version by another. This action requires defining a deployment process. This deployment must be accompanied by a software application's deployment (SDM) manual.

The deployment of a new version can lead to different situations as follows:

– everything goes well (this is rarely the case);

– the equipment configuration (equipment, system, etc.) is not that which is referenced in the documents and the deployment fails (bad reaction, inability to start, etc.);

– the installation of the previous version software is not correct (different files, written protected files, moved files, directories having a different name, directories that are not provided for in the tree, etc.), making it difficult to install the new version and possibly leading to a wrong execution (wrong library used, etc.).

The SDM manual must identify the following:

– the version of the software to deploy;

– the loading process of the version;

– the verification process to verify that the version has actually been loaded (verification by self-identification of the software);

– the verification process to verify that the loaded version functions correctly in the current environment. Therefore, identify a number of tests of correct functioning and there will be a production of formalized trial results in the deployment manual;

– the rollback process: if a problem does not allow the system to function properly with the new version, the ability to return to the initial configuration should be present;

– the configuration updating process of the equipment. The update can be documentary (system folder, train folder, etc.), electronic (modification of database, etc.), etc.

The deployment of software therefore requires the production of different documents:

– a software application deployment plan (SDP) that will describe the method of deployments and measures to be implemented to manage this activity;

– a software application deployment manual (SDM) that shows the process for a given version;

– a software application deployment register (SDR) that contains the results of a given deployment.

As already indicated, every activity having been verified, it is necessary to produce a software deployment verification report (SD-VR), which shows that the productions of the deployment activity have been verified.

10.4. In reality

The CENELEC EN 50128:2011 standard was right to introduce this chapter on the deployment of new versions of a software application, but the deployment of a new version is rarely directed by the industrialist that has realized the system. Also, the manufacturer will be able to provide the SDP, SDM and SVS but there is only very little chance that he/she can retrieve the deployment records and finalize his/her report on deployment verification (SD-VR).

A manufacturer will therefore have to consider as deployed a version that has been sent to his/her client. Note that it would be wise to complete the deployment records with a deployment register (SDR) that will allow the manufacturer to know all the versions considered as deployed.

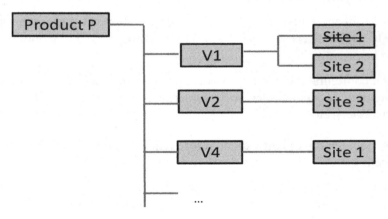

Figure 10.1. *SDR*

Figure 10.1 presents an example of an SDR; we can see that there are three versions of the same software application deployed on three sites and that version 3 was never deployed. We also see that site 1 has changed from version 1 to version 4. This information is useful to identify compatibility problems in the event of a major development, and to identify the previous version in case of a need to return to a previous version.

Meanwhile, the system's head of operations shall implement a configuration management process, save the items provided by the industrial and establish a deployment process that will produce the requested items.

10.5. Conclusion

In this chapter we presented deployment, which is an important issue beginning to emerge as one of the points that is most difficult to control. Part of the complexity is induced by the increase in the amount of software used within a system, which when coupled with the number of known defects, causes the number of identified hardware configurations to become a real problem.

The parameterization and the concept of product line introduce a level of complexity that seeks to introduce a real configuration management but also seeks to identify the versions already installed.

The management of changes, configuration, maintenance and deployment is a set that must be mastered, and to do this, processes, plans and especially training must be implemented.

Verification and Validation

11.1. Introduction

This chapter is designed to introduce the concepts, techniques and to a lesser extent the implemented tools to verify and validate a software-based system. It is about seeing the verification as a support process with methods that are independent of the product to realize.

Verification and validation (V&V) activities are essential for the realization of a software application that reaches a particular confidence level. The V&V is a set of activities that extends throughout the implementation cycle.

In this chapter, we are placed in the context of a software realization process that is based on a V cycle (see Figure 11.1) as advocated by the standards applicable to safety-operating systems (Generic IEC 61508 [IEC 08], Rail CENELEC EN 50128 [CEN 01, CEN 11], Aeronautics DO178 [RTA 92, RTA 11], Nuclear [IEC 06] and Automotive ISO 26262 [ISO 11]).

The realization of a software application must take into account the design of the software application, but it must also take into account activities to demonstrate that the software application reaches a certain level of quality. The achievement of a quality level passes through the demonstration that no defect has been introduced during the design and that the product meets the needs that have been identified.

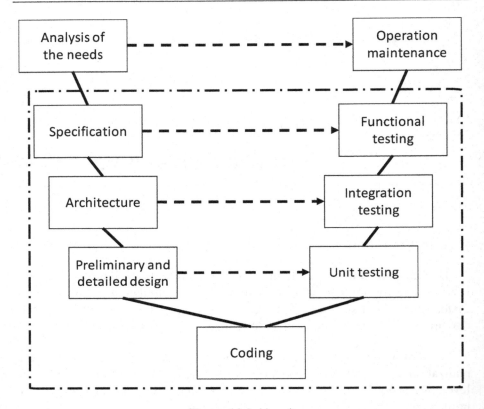

Figure 11.1. *V cycle*

The V cycle (see Figure 11.1), usually used for the realization of software application, reveals the verification activities by tests in the ascendant phase, but it is necessary to add all reviews and analyses from the documentation and/or the code.

11.2. Concept

11.2.1. *Introduction*

First and foremost, we must remember the definition of V&V.

DEFINITION 11.1.– (VERIFICATION). *Confirmation by tangible evidence that the specified requirements have been met at every stage of the realization process.*

DEFINITION 11.2.– (VALIDATION). *Confirmation by tangible evidence that the requirements for a specific use or planned application have been met by the final product.*

The two definitions above are extracted from the standard ISO 9000:2000 (see [ISO 00]). They introduce the requirement concepts and notions of evidence. To be more precise, we can resume the presentation made by Sommerville (see [SOM 07]).

In 1979, Boehm stated that:

– verification ensures that the product conforms to its specification;

– validation ensures that the system implemented corresponds to the expectations of the future user.

By definition, validation therefore aims to demonstrate the suitability of the product with the original need.

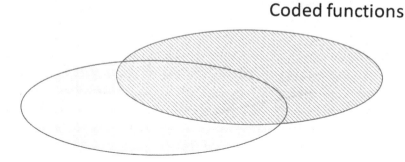

Coded functions

Specified functions

Figure 11.2. *Issue of software development*

Figure 11.2 shows the main issue of the realization of a software application. Indeed, there is a need to achieve and there is a realization, verification is there to show that all of the need is taken into account by the realization and that there is no unpredicted element. The development team will always have a good reason to introduce unwanted code pieces (functions to reuse, addition of service, etc.) and to not take into account all of the needs (technical difficulties, forgetfulness, etc.).

In view of the definitions, we can conclude (see Figure 11.3) that verification applies to all stages of the V cycle and that validation is an activity which aims to show that the specification is respected by the final product. This concerns the functional tests, also called validation tests.

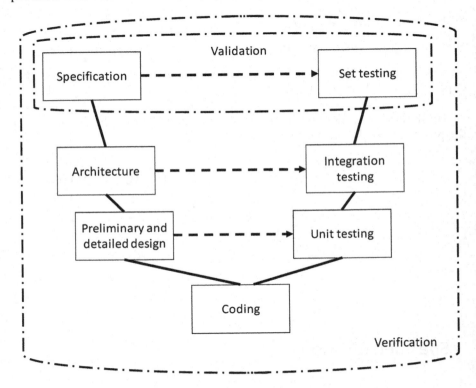

Figure 11.3. *Positioning of V&V on the V cycle*

Standard ISO 9001:2015 [ISO 15] recommends that each production be systematically verified. Standard CENELEC EN 50128:2011 reinforces this point by indicating that the role of verification is to show that the product is being achieved correctly (no introduction of defects). That is why, as shown in Figure 11.3, verification is an activity that covers every phase of the lifecycle.

As shown in Figure 11.3, verification concerns the search for defects within the V cycle, and validation concerns the demonstration that the product meets its need. That is why its location is at the higher level of the V cycle; verification covers validation.

11.2.2. *Verification*

11.2.2.1. *Presentation*

In the context of the standard IEC 61508 (see [IEC 08]), "verification" is the activity that consists, for each phase of the lifecycle (general, hardware and software), of demonstrating by analysis and/or trial that, for specific entries, the deliverables meet in every way the objectives and prescriptions (requirements) set for the phase. As shown in Figure 11.4, on the basis of inputs and activities, we need to show that the elements of outputs are correct.

In addition to the items discussed previously, we must indicate the need to have elements of evidence that allow demonstrating that the verification activity has been properly conducted, and that the product meets the entry requirements (from definition 11.1).

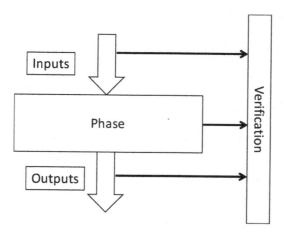

Figure 11.4. *Verification*

Verification of a phase requires analyzing the implementation of the quality requirements (application of procedures, respect of formats, etc.), the application of processes (compliance of plans, respect of the organization, etc.), the correction of activities and taking due account of the safety requirements:

> *Verification is designed to show that the product has been properly achieved. The associated question is therefore: is the work well done?*

11.2.2.2. Verification activity

It is possible to say that verification is the activity that consists, for each phase of the lifecycle, of demonstrating by analysis and/or trial that, for specific entries, the deliverables meet the objectives in every way (as identified in the plans) and the requirements for the phase. Here is a non-exhaustive list of verification activities:

– the reviews related to the outputs of a phase (documents relating to all phases of the safety lifecycle) destined to ensure compliance with the objectives and requirements of the phase, and taking into account the specific entries at this phase;

– design reviews: code analysis, verification of encoding rules, etc.;

– general tests made on the products in order to ensure that their operation complies with their specification;

– integration tests performed during the element-by-element assembly of different parts of a system, from environmental testing, to ensure that all parts function with each other in accordance with the specifications;

– the components test done after the completion of a component; at this point in the presentation, we will make the link between components tests and modules test and/or unit test.

Verification is a process that takes care of the implementation phases, and carries on:

– the system's structure, how it is made, with reference to standards and the properties to satisfy (verify the product);

– the means used, and the production process; with reference to rules on the work method, and how to proceed (verify the process).

Verification is designed to show that the product is well achieved. The notion of a "well-achieved product" means that no defect has been introduced during the phases associated with the achievement.

There are two types of verification:

– static verification, which does not require the execution of all or part of the scanned system;

– dynamic verification, based on the execution of all or part of the scanned system.

In addition to the verification of the product, the verification of the quality of the product should not be forgotten, and it will be directed by the quality team through quality audit (on the product, on the project or on the application of a process), through a review of produced elements (documentation, etc.) and control activities (monitoring of anomalies, monitoring of non-conformities, monitoring of customer returns, etc.).

11.2.3. *Validation*

Validation in the context of a system's lifecycle includes activities that ensure and build trust in the system and its ability to meet intended uses to achieve the goals and objectives assigned.

In the standard IEC 61508 [IEC 08], the "validation" is the activity that consists of demonstrating that the system, before or after installation, corresponds to the requirements contained in the specification of this system. Thus, for example, the validation of the software consists of the confirmation, by examination and provision of objective evidence, that the software meets the specification of the software's requirements of safety.

As shown in Figure 11.5, validation is an activity that allows us to show that the software application renders the planned service. The planned service being defined by the requirements; it is necessary to show that the software application on the target hardware realizes the requirements through a testing activity. If we consider the test activity as a verification activity, the validation is the confirmation, by examination and provision of objective evidence, that the software meets the specification of the software's safety requirements. Validation consists of showing the achievement of the right product.

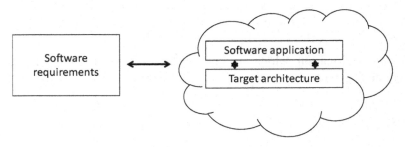

Figure 11.5. *Validation*

11.3. Techniques, methods and practices

In this section, we present the different techniques and methods associated with the V&V. The presentation of the techniques will be limited to the strictly necessary; it is to be noted that certain techniques will be analyzed more in detail in more specialized chapters.

11.3.1. *Static verification*

11.3.1.1. *Presentation*

The static verification is based on the absence of execution of all or part of the system. The absence of execution allows achieving this type of analysis at any stage of the realization process (specification, design, coding, testing, etc.). The static verification may be manual or using equipment.

A few qualities expected of the code, a "piece of code" (portion of code, procedure, program, file, etc.), must be:

– commented;

– readable;

– modular;

– of mastered complexity;

– in compliance with the design file.

11.3.1.2. *Manual static analysis*

In this section, we present two manual static analysis techniques that are software inspection and software effects errors analysis (SEEA).

11.3.1.2.1. Software inspection – principles

Software inspection (see [GRA 93]) is the manual static analysis technique that aims to discover defects at the earliest.

DEFINITION 11.3.– (SOFTWARE INSPECTION). *Software inspection is a control technique for ensuring that the documentation produced during a given phase remains consistent with the documentation of the previous phases and respects preestablished rules and standards.*

The purpose of software inspection is to look for defects (of understanding, interpretation, translation, etc.), deviations, especially regarding quality clauses, absences or abundances etc., and to provide the elements to make corrections. Software inspection is not designed to make corrections. In order to be effective, software inspection must be prepared and carried out by a separate team from the realization team.

Software inspection is divided into two types of inspection/review:

– the document inspection/review: we are interested in the documents produced for a given phase. The inspection will focus on the quality, the correctness and the relevance of the document(s);

– the inspection/review of the code: there is interest in the items of type "computer file": model, program source files, test scenarios, etc.

11.3.1.2.2. Documentary inspection

The documentary inspection will verify:

– that quality instructions described in the company's repository (QAM, procedure, standards and applicable repositories) and project plans (QAP, SQAP, SVVP, SCMP)[1] were taken into account;

---

1 Quality assurance plan, software quality assurance plan, verification and validation plan, safety assurance plan, and configuration management plan.

– the correction of the work accomplished; this requires knowing the entries of the phase, the process to be conducted and having control points (checklist to implement);

– the compliance (relevance) of the work; at the end of the documentary inspection, a formal review (meeting of the people implied in the inspection) must allow deciding on the conformity of the work.

In the context of documentary inspection, anomalies can be detected and reported.

11.3.1.2.3. Code inspection

Code inspection will verify the:

– respect of the programming rules;

– readability;

– presence and pertinence of the comments;

– compliance of code/file of the design.

To accomplish the code review, a referential is needed:

– standard to meet;

– business standards;

– coding standards;

– quality procedures.

A review process which will be described by a quality procedure for example and which is based on control lists (questions to ask, points to consider, etc.), and above all having a goal of the code review.

Code inspection in the case of safety is called critical code review (CCR); it is an activity that involves reviewing the entirety or part of the code of a software application. This reviewing process covers at least four objectives:

– verify the conformance of code with project documentation such as software design documents required to describe data handling, types, algorithms and traceability with requirements that the component review must comply with;

– verify the proper implementation of barriers and protections that have been identified to be implemented;

– verify that the programming rules are respected;

– verify that the identified requirements related to safety are correctly implemented.

Here are some examples of rules to verify:

– naming rules: every object has a name that follows its category-specific syntax, for example C_xx, V_xx, T_xx;

– typing rules: any object is typed (no default typing);

– rule of initialization: any declared object is initialized;

– rule of use: any data produced is consumed.

One of the difficulties related to programming is the fact that programming languages are not perfect, and hence we must take a subset of a language and define specific protections in the form of programming rules.

Programming rules are composed of:

– rules for naming objects to increase readability;

– rules related to typing; standards recommending the use of a strong typing language and the choice of a language like C that requires addition of defensive programming to restrict the objects to functional type as defined in the specifications;

– rules prohibiting certain constructions (e.g. do not use pointers) or recommending specific forms to protect certain construction (in case of use of pointer verify before and after use);

– rules exported by reused elements and/or preexisting components;

– rules exported by execution platform (safety related application constraints) and/or by the operating system.

CCR is generally formalized as:

– a form (checklist) that requires identification of a component, its version, level of safety and document repository to be taken into consideration;

– a table listing the programming rules with an evaluation of whether the rule is applicable, or properly applied and where in the case of faults there will be a justification or a link to fault report.

CCR is a manual activity based on types of tools; editor, text processing, etc., but it can also rely on verification tools of programming rules such as *codewizard*.

11.3.1.2.4. Software error effects analysis

While developing the very first applications for metro such as SACEM [NF 90, GAR 94], several questions were raised regarding the impact of software errors on the complete system. This elicited two type of responses (for more information, see [THI 86]):

– establishment of the safety architecture to detect random faults and/or the process (compile, download, etc.) through implementation of safe coded processor;

– minimize systematic errors of the software through formal implementation.

Software effects error (SEEA) [AFN 90, GAR 94] is part of the analyses that are made at various stages of development. SEEA consists of examining the consequences of potential software errors.

The objectives of SEEA (see also Volume 1 [BOU 16]) are as follows:

– to accurately identify these integrated software components, and to assess their level of criticality;

– to propose measures to detect defects and to improve the robustness of the software;

– to evaluate the level of validation effort to be performed on the various components of the software.

Its application is categorized into three phases:

– preliminary analysis of all the safety procedures to characterize the deepening of studies for each procedure (from safety objectives, the identification of the procedures is made);

– procedure by procedure analysis, the consequences of the safety of the proposed software errors (analysis sheet of each procedure analyzed by identification of errors, safety criteria associated with each error and the consequences);

– work synthesis regarding the validation of the software and the development of the safety file (list of scenarios contrary to safety, identified safety criteria, proposed means of detection).

Analysis of software error effects							
Name of program: Calculator: Language:				Realized by: Date: Last version:			
Module	Function	Error	Error type	Effect on the component	Effect on the system	Preventative measure	Remarks

Figure 11.6. *Example of an SEEA table*

Some SEEAs have been, for the first time, carried out in the context of the validation of Line D of the automatic metro in Lyon, France named MAGGALY (in English, "wide-gauge metro of Lyon's agglomeration", see [MAI 93]). These first SEEAs have brought on the code, but in the context of the realization of the automatic metro named SAET-METEOR (line 14 of the Paris metro, see [CHA 96, MAT 98], where SAET is, in English, "system of automation of the exploitation of trains"), they were carried out both on code and on specifications.

SEEA therefore allows analyzing the impact of a failure of a function's input on an output, both on the specification level and the code level.

Regarding the aspects of systems, subsystems, equipment and/or materials, there is a study implemented in the framework of safe-functioning activities called failure modes and effects analysis (FMEA). FMEA is a method of preventive analysis that identifies and highlights the potential risks. It is a systematic study (for more information, see [GAR 94]). SEEA is the equivalent of the FMEA. The main feature of these studies is that they are purely "manual" and that the only tools required are a word processor or a spreadsheet.

In general, the SEEA is considered to be a safety study but under the standards CENELEC EN 50128 [CEN 01, CEN 11], IEC 62279 [IEC 14], IEC 61508 [IEC 08], etc. The SEEAs are seen as verification activities.

The approach presented above is a general approach and currently we use a specific SEEA for each industry. As a general rule, SEEA is carried out to avoid propagation of faults over the rest of the software application as it involves significant costs to study, which could be as much as for creating a fault tree. Certain industries carry out SEEA to confirm the level of criticality of functions/modules/components constituting the software application.

Finally, we must remember that as SEEA involves analyzing the code, it is interesting to use it along with CCR.

SEEA is a very interesting approach for analyzing the architecture of a software application or its code. It helps to cover the following points:

– identification of gaps in the architecture and/or the code and the impact on the system;

– identification of barriers and protections to be implemented;

– justification of barriers and protections by introducing a link on failures and their impact on the system;

– identification of the consequences of failure on other components and the software application;

– justification for the classification of failures;

– identification of additional verifications.

SEEA has been implemented in the context of software applications with varying degrees of success. Note that the standards CENELEC EN 50128, ISO 26262 and IEC 61508 recommend the implementation of SEEA. The standard CENELEC EN 50128 recommends the implementation of SEEA to verify an architecture and the code.

11.3.1.3. *Static analysis*

11.3.1.3.1. Introduction

First of all, it is necessary to define a static analyzer:

DEFINITION 11.4.– (STATIC ANALYZER) [ISO 85]. *Software tool analyzing the structure and the text of a program without the execution of it: loops, inaccessible parts, redundancies, etc.*

A static analyzer allows verifying the interfaces, identifying the incorrect constructions, uninitialized variables, out-of-standard program parts and generating certain software documentation (cross references, diagram, etc.).

In the following, we will present different types of tool static analysis: compiler, program static analysis, metric construction, abstract program interpretation, etc.

11.3.1.3.2. Compilation

A standard compiler is divided into several phases:

– syntactic analysis;

– typing phase;

– semantic analysis;

– generation of the executable.

Compilers are tools that perform a number of verification activities on the source code of an application.

DEFINITION 11.5.– (COMPILER). *Software tool used to translate a software design, expressed in a programming language, into a code that can be executed by the hardware.*

Compilers have specific options that allow obtaining information on the analyzed program:

– cross-reference table;

– size of the executable (code, data);

– address table of the data.

Some languages such as C are partially "ill defined", hence the need to make additional corrections to that of the compiler. Language C is one of those languages. Initially, the LINT tool has been designed to verify the latent errors related to typing, function calls, etc. This tool has been extended to other languages (see the pcLint tool).

11.3.1.3.3. Identification of differences

The control of the evolution of an application goes through the analysis of the differences between two versions of the software. The basic tools are fairly simple, such as the unix diff command, for example.

11.3.1.3.4. Verification of encoding rules

Control of the quality of the development and properties such as the readability and maintainability goes through the implementation of a set of programming and architectural rules that must be respected throughout all the realization process. The different standards recommend formalizing the rules of programming and coding in the form of a guide.

Programming and coding rules should cover different areas:

– formatting rules;

– definition of good practice rules;

– definition of the language subset rules.

Table 11.1 introduces a sample table allowing the description of programming and coding rules. Table 11.2 presents some MISRA-C rules.

Rule name	A unique identifier for each rule
SIL level	Each rule can be associated with one or more levels of safety: SSIL0/SSIL2/SSIL4
Description	The description of the rule can be the text used in the standard
Explanation	The description can be very brief and an explanation can facilitate understanding
Examples	For each rule, it is necessary to introduce at least one example of correct use and a counterexample
Type	This attribute is designed to indicate if the rule is mandatory (*required*) or recommended (*advisory*) It is possible to define more to identify rules that have an impact on the form or other aspects
Verification	Types of verifications to implement: proofreading, tools, etc.
Traceability	Here we trace with different standards: – MISRA-C; – MISRA-C++; – CENELEC 50128; – JSF++.
Impact	Here, it will be indicated that the impact can take place with the non-compliance of the rule: safety impact, testability impact, verification impact, maintainability impact, etc.

Table 11.1. *Example of description of the rules*

MISRA-C [MIS 04] specifies some programming rules (see the examples in Table 1.3), making it possible to avoid execution errors as a result of poorly defined constructions, unforeseen behaviors (certain C language structures are not completely defined) and misunderstandings between those in charge of production (legible code, code with implicit, etc.). Several tools enable the MISRA-C rules to be automatically verified.

The MISRA-C [MIS 04] standard repeats some rules that are explicit in several standards (see, for example, 14.4 and 14.7):

– rule 14.4: Table A.12, in the EN 50128 standard or Table B.1 in the IEC 61508 standard;

– rule 14.7: Table A.20, in the EN 50128 standard or Table B.9 in the IEC 61508 standard.

MISRA-C [MIS 98] was created in 1998 and updated in 2004 [MIS 04], which shows that some experience feedback has been made use of.

Id	Status	Description
Rule 1.1	Required	All of the code must conform to the ISO 9899:1990 norm "Programming languages – C", amended and corrected by ISO/IEC9899/COR1:1995, ISO/IEC/9899/AMD1:1995 and ISO/IEC9899/COR2:1996.
Rule 5.4	Required	Each tag is a single identifier.
Rule 14.1	Required	There must not be any dead code.
Rule 14.4	Required	No unconditional jumps (goto) in programs.
Rule 14.7	Required	A function must have a single output point at the end of the function.
Rule 17.1	Required	The pointer arithmetic can only be used for pointers which address a table or tabular element.
Rule 17.5	Advisory	An object declaration must not contain more than two levels of pointer indirection.

Table 11.2. *Some MISRA-C: 2004 [MIS 04] rules*[2]

Metric	Maximum threshold
Maximum number of rows in C files	2,000
Comment rate in C files	40%
Maximum number of a function's exit points	1
Maximum number of *gotos*	0
Maximum number of operations out of reach	0

Table 11.3. *Example of verified metric as rules for programming*

The verification of these rules must be automated to consider tools such as LDRA, QCA, etc. It is important to have an automatic process because

---

2 [MIS 04] introduces 122 "required" and 20 "advisory" rules.

the rules can be complex and, in view of the size of the code, it is not reasonable to analyze it completely by hand.

These programming rules can be induced by constraints of enterprises, compliance with specific repository (for example MISRAC [MIS 04, MIS 12]) and/or known problems (semantics problem, readability problem, no determinism, bad constructions, etc.; see section 11.3.1.2.1).

Table 11.3 shows metrics that will be associated with encoding rules and that will be verified as encoding rules.

11.3.1.3.5. Quality of a software application

There are quality criteria dedicated to code that are interesting to know, such as:

– the readability of a function represents its ability to quickly render the information it contains. This criterion depends on the complexity of the control graph, the length of the function and the average size of its instructions;

– the simplicity of a function is its ability to present and perform simple actions. This criterion depends on the structure of the function, the number of the function's instructions and the average size of its instructions;

– the testability of a function represents its ability to be testable. This criterion depends on the structuring of the function, the complexity of the control graph (see section 11.3.1.2.7) and the number of direct calls of functions within the function.

The previously identified criteria can be associated with metrics that must be applied to the code.

11.3.1.3.6. Measure of the complexity

Control of a software application requires mastery of the code's complexity. The complexity of the code is an indicator used to validate objectives related to quality to assess the effort of tests, and to evaluate the maintainability and reliability of the code. The complexity of the code is a measure.

DEFINITION 11.6.– (MEASURE). *A formula that allows evaluating a quality from various measurable parameters.*

DEFINITION 11.7.– (METRIC). *A metric is composed of a measure and a theory of the measure on the space on which we measure.*

In our case, the theory of measurement [HAB 91] consists of defining the limits to respect in the project (or the company) and the principles of interpretation (see Table 11.4).

Metric	Common abbreviation	Maximum threshold
Number of function calls	CALL	7
Cyclomatic number	VG	30
Average size of instructions	AVGS	20
Maximum nesting level	NEST	7
Length of the function	N	1,000
Number of instructions per function	STMT	100
Number of parameters passed to functions		8

Table 11.4. *Example of basic metrics*

Here are some measures (see, for example, [CAB 96]):

– *Cyclomatic number v(G)*: The cyclomatic number describes the complexity of a program. It allows quantifying the number of execution ways of a procedure/function. This metric is measured from the control graph (see section 11.3.1.2.7).

– *Number of code lines*: There are several variations (with or without commentary, with or without the white line). This metric allows evaluating readability and maintainability (presence of comment).

– *Halstead metrics*: This collection of metrics allows evaluating the complexity of a piece of program through the complexity of expressions (operators and operands).

– Number of errors detected, number of errors corrected and evolution number.

It is important to note that it is possible to build direct metrics (relating to the code) or indirect metrics (synthesis of other metrics, analysis of the process, etc.).

For example, Table 11.5 shows an example of a metrics results measure on a code through the "Logiscope" tool. The table shows the name of the metric, the terminals of min and max (chosen for the project or the company) and the measure that has been made.

0	Mnemonic	Low	High	Value
Number of statements	N_STMTS	1	50	70
Program length	PR_LGTH	3	350	85
Cyclomatic number	VG	1	20	11
Max. no. of levels	MAX_LVLS	1	5	3
No. of non-cyclic paths	N_PATHS	1	80	29
Number of jumps	N_JUMPS	0	0	0
Comments frequency	COM_R	0.2	1.0	0.17
Average statement size	AVG_S	3	7	1.21
No. of I/O points	IO_PTS	2	2	2

Table 11.5. *Example of a table containing the result of metrics measurement*

On the basis of basic metrics, it is possible to build metrics linked to quality criteria as shown in Table 11.5. R_xxxx takes the value 1 if the metric respects the terminal and 0 otherwise. So, therefore, the three criteria have a maximum value of 12 if all metrics are respected and 0 in the worst cases. The weight placed on the metrics allows reinforcing certain metrics essential to a criterion. For example, for testability, the number of tests is an essential metric; this is why the weight value is 6.

Metrics	Definition
Testability	6*R_VG + 3*R_CALL + 3*R_NEST
Simplicity	6*R_VG + 3*R_AVGS + 3*R_STMT
Readability	4*R_AVGS + 4*R_N + 4*R_NEST

Table 11.6. *Example of complex metrics*

Concerning the applicability of the theory of the measure in the context of object-oriented languages, there is, for the moment, no answer. Some metrics are related to the object oriented application, but these metrics focus on the structure and it is difficult to put them in relation with the traditional quality indicators (test effort, maintainability, etc.).

11.3.1.3.7. Structural analysis

The structural analysis of a program P is to construct an oriented graph. This graph can be used to analyze the flood of data, measure the structural complexity or study the ways of execution.

The oriented graph provides a compact view of the control structure of the program P being analyzed:

– it is built from the source code of the program;

– a node = maximum block of consecutive instructions $i_1,\ldots,i_n$;

    - i_1 is the single access point of the bloc,

    - instructions are always executed in order $i_1,\ldots,i_n$,

    - the block is left after execution of i_n,

– a single entry node, one or more exit nodes;

– arcs between the nodes = connections that are conditional or unconditional.

The control graph (see Figure 11.7) allows visualizing the structure of a program and identifying the critical points. It allows calculating the structural metrics (e.g. cyclomatic number).

The main anomalies encountered are (non-exhaustive list) as follows:

– isolated components (in general never called – be careful nonetheless of the components used by graphical interfaces);

– level breaks;

– a call graph is structured in hierarchical levels that must be respected;

– a multilevel break indicates a poor design of the software application;

– graph too large (bad hierarchical decomposition);

– graph too deep;

– spaghetti bowl (links in all directions, inability to isolate a component, etc.).

```
void main()
{
    int x = 0;
    int y = 1;
    while (y < 10)
    {
        y = 2 * y;
        x = x + 1;
    }
    printf ("%d",x);
    printf ("%d",y);
}
```

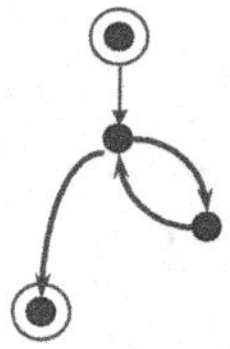

Figure 11.7. *Example of a control graph*

The software application was divided into small components that may no longer have specific features and it may also cause problems at the time of integration tests.

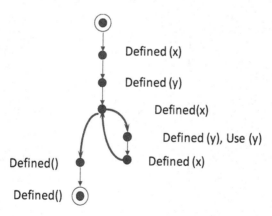

Figure 11.8. *Analysis of the data flow*

The control graph can be annotated to study the flow of data as shown in Figure 11.8.

The detectable anomalies from data flows are mainly:

– usage of a variable without prior assignment;

– assignment of a variable without further use;

– redefinition of a variable without having used it first.

The control graph is a synthesis of a program that can be analyzed from multiple angles in order to understand the complexity, the testability (sequence of branches and paths) and even to identify the anomalies.

11.3.1.3.8. Symbolic execution

From a software application P, the symbolic evaluation builds symbolic expressions linking the entry data E to the output data O. These expressions also include some conditions in order to follow a certain path during the execution.

Symbolic execution is to perform an execution of a software application but by changing the type of data. Indeed, we have passed from a software application that manipulates numbers to a manipulation of algebraic expressions. The complete symbolic execution of a software application is impossible; as a limit, the number of revolutions of the loops is often dependent on the execution.

	X0	**Y0**
Begin	X0-Y0	Y0
x := x-y;	X0 –Y0	Y0+X0–Y0
y := y+x;		X0
x := y-x;		
End	X0 – (X0-Y0)	X0
	Y0	

Figure 11.9. *Example of symbolic execution*

11.3.1.3.9. Abstract program interpretation

Abstract interpretation [COU 00, BOU 11] is a technique of automatic static analysis. Abstract interpretation consists of replacing a precise element of a program by a less detailed abstraction hoping to calculate the properties of this program. Abstraction leads to a loss of safe information that leads to not knowing how to conclude on all the programs.

The abstract interpretation of a program allows detecting the execution errors (runtime error) such as division by 0, overflow… but also defects of access to shared variables and dead code. The great advantage of these tools is that the test is carried out without any preparation from the sources of the project. If we make a comparison with the costs of unit tests, the argument is significant.

There are two main uses of abstract interpretation:

– recipe of the final product;

- the supervisor can use the abstract interpretation for a recipe of the code provided by the manufacturer,

– debugging of the product under development;

- during development, the developers use abstract interpretation to detect design anomalies (unit tests),

- the verification team can use it to detect the shadow areas to be examined in priority.

11.3.1.3.10. Modeling

The realization of a model M is a way to understand and/or apprehend a problem/situation. In general, the specification phase that allows adapting the specifications goes through the creation of a model M.

The static view (Figure 11.10) has two points of view: the hierarchical point of view that allows visualizing the decomposition tree, and the composition point of view that allows visualizing the communications between modules of the same level; this promotes the black box vision of the modules.

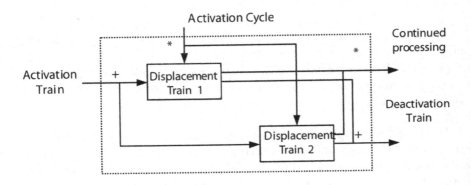

Figure 11.10. *Example of static introducing different types of communication*

Figure 11.11 shows an example of a dynamic model in the form of a states/transitions diagram.

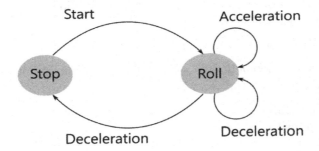

Figure 11.11. *Example of a model*

Modeling often relies on a graphic representation of the system that is described in the form of a tree structure of separate and autonomous entities which communicate with each other and with the environment of the system. The first models were based on functional analyses of the system (see the work around structured analysis and design technique (SADT)[3] [LIS 90]).

---

3 This method has been developed by the company Softech in the USA. The SADT method is a method of analysis by successive levels of descriptive approach of a whole, whatever it may be.

A model can be more or less close to the studied system, referred to as abstraction. The closer the modeling, the more similar the results will be to those that will be observed on the final system. Another feature of the models is that the language support features, or not, semantics. The presence of semantics allows implementing reasoning techniques that ensure the correction of the results obtained.

Two complementary models are frequently used with this specification:

– a static model describing the entities constituting the system and the states that can be associated with them;

– a dynamic model describing the authorized state changes.

Model M describes the behavior of the system:

– states/transitions system;

– logical equations;

Model M has access to data:

– controllable (known, fixed, etc.);

– probabilistic.

In an overall manner, modeling consists of translating a physical situation into a symbolic model in a more or less abstract language of iconic type (graphic symbols: tables, curves, diagrams, etc.) or of logico-mathematic type (function, relation, etc.).

As an example, the unified modeling language (UML)[4] notation [OMG 06a, OMG 06b] is a way to make a model (see Figure 11.12). Using UML notation is thus not without certain questions [BOU 07, OKA 07]. How to use a notation without a semantic? How to evaluate an application based on UM notation? etc. Several works aim to offer answers to these questions [OOT 04, MOT 05].

---

4 For more information, visit the website of the Object Management Group (OMG). http://www.omg.org/.

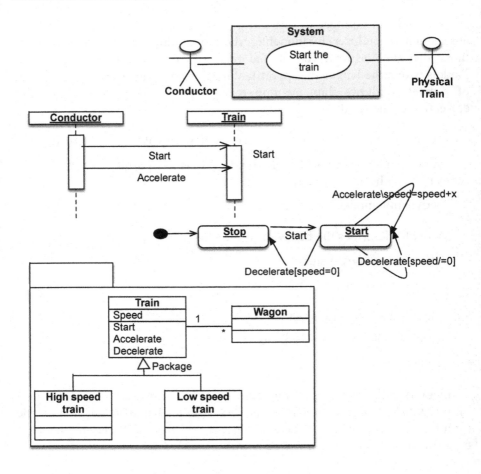

Figure 11.12. *Example of model UML*

For the moment, UML notation [OMG 06a, OMG 06b, OMG 07] is not recognized as a structured and/or semiformal method in the standards, even if many would like to implement it completely or partially.

In [BOU 07], [BOU 09a] and Chapter 19 of [RAM 09], we have shown how UML notation can be used to create some models of safety-critical systems.

11.3.1.3.11. Simulation

From a model of the product to be analyzed, it is possible to carry out behavior analyses through interactive simulation (or automatic) and/or exhaustive simulation (model checking).

DEFINITION 11.8.– (SIMULATION). *The simulation of a model M corresponds to achieving a controlled execution of this model.*

The purpose of the simulation is as follows:

– understand the workings of a complex system;

– put properties in evidence;

  - safety,

  - performance,

– perform experiments;

  - difficult, for example nuclear explosion,

  - expensive, for example biological experimentation,

  - impossible, for example modeling of a system under interpretation.

– validate the specifications;

– validate the behavior.

The simulation may be carried out in a loop until a termination has been requested following the diagram:

– choice of entries;

– execution of a calculation step;

– recovery of the outputs.

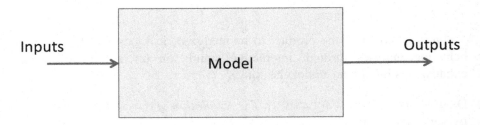

Figure 11.13. *Model without environment (open loop)*

In the context of simulation, the entries of the model are variables from an environment. There are two cases: either there is an environment or it is absent. In the absence of an environment model, the entries must be selected manually (randomly at worst). There are two problems that then arise:

– consistency between the various entries;

– link between the outputs and the state of the model.

The establishment of an environment involves a complementary development and validation efforts in order to demonstrate the validity of this environment.

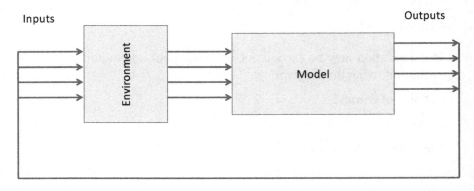

Figure 11.14. *Model with environment (closed loop)*

Regarding simulation, there are three possibilities:

– *"Step by step" simulation*: The model is executed step by step (interactive), and the user chooses the transitions to execute among those which are "stretchable":

  - there is always an initial state,

  - a transition is said to be "stretchable" if the beginning state is active, the associated event to the transition is produced and if the associated condition to the transition is true;

– *"Automatic" simulation*: A process chooses the transitions to execute among those that are "stretchable". There may be a taking into account of the environment through a modeling of it. The choice of transitions remains the delicate point: "computing coincidence".

– *"Exhaustive" simulation* (model checking): Construction of the graph of all possible executions and then it is possible to reason about the graph:

  - verification of property,

  - search for subtrees,

  - selection of test cases.

Exhaustive simulation [BAI 08] allows automatically verifying the properties of a model. The implementation of an exhaustive simulation needs semantics and is based on the usage of a temporal logic to express the properties.

The properties that can be verified can be classified into families:

– *Safety properties*: A property that is always true in all states announcing that certain things will never happen (for example there is no train collision);

– *Liveness properties*: A property that is possibly true in some states introducing that certain things will happen (including the good things) (for example if we call the elevator, it will arrive in the near future).

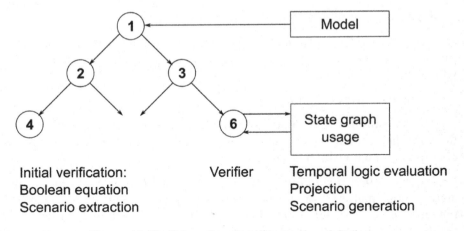

Figure 11.15. *Exhaustive simulation and exploitation*

The main difficulty of implementing exhaustive simulation resides in the mastering of the memory size of the graph of states of the system being analyzed. We are very often confronted with the problem of the combinatorial explosion: the number of states of the system is too high.

Thus, there are many solutions:

– implement optimization algorithms of the size of the graph in memory, for example the *binary decision diagram*;

– implement an abstraction of the model;

– implement an analysis strategy of the system based on trajectories (partial analysis);

– implement other strategies of state management, for example we may no longer memorize the states but we may memorize the properties of these states.

11.3.1.3.12. Model for verification

From a program P, its specification SP and a set A of safety properties on P expressed in the form of variables expression of P, it is possible to build a model M that has for entry E and for output the Boolean S and S'.

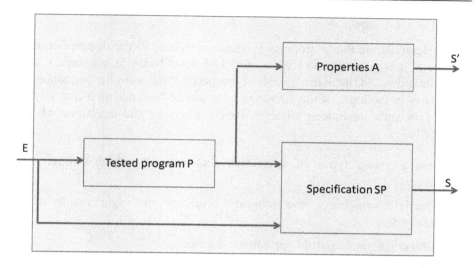

Figure 11.16. *Example of verification principle*

The formal verification of a program P then simulates (interactively or exhaustively) the model with entries in order to verify that we always have the functioning output (Figure 11.16).

To facilitate the verification phase, it is preferable to carry out the closure of the model by introducing an environment that allows generating the entries and reacting to the outputs. The dynamic behavior of such a model in its environment is represented in Figure 11.11.

Examples of safety properties applicable to the system SAET-METEOR (see [BOU 06]) are as follows:

– *P1*: Only trains that are equipped, localized and have an automatic driving mode can have a target;

– *P2*: The internal state of the AP-Line representing the occupancy of the path must be consistent with all of the trains (equipped or not) present in the zone managed by this AP-Line.

In [BOU 99], we have shown how the realization of a model based on the principles, as shown in Figure 11.12, can verify a textual specification and select validation tests.

11.3.1.3.13. Evidence

To demonstrate that a property P is true compared to the description of a system S, it is necessary to have a model M described in a language L that has semantics. Mathematic proof of property P is a finite sequence of inferences in the logic of the language L. It should be noted first that formal proof is a static technique since it does not require the execution of the model M.

There are two types of correction that can be studied through the evidence:

– partial correctness: the program produces the right result if its execution ends;

– total correctness: partial correctness + ending.

Evidence techniques are based on the triplets of Hoare (see [HOA 69]). Intuitively, the triplet {P} S {Q} (P and Q are predicates characterizing the state of the system's variables and S a piece of program) has the following meaning: "if P is correct before executing S, and if S terminates, then Q is correct after".

It is therefore possible, through the rules of use of the triplets of Hoare [HOA 69], to implement reasoning (inference set), which allows demonstrating the correctness of the program. Currently, the manipulation rules of the triplets are expressed through "sequent".

For example, the sequent in Figure 11.17 indicates that to run in sequence S1 and S2 going from P and to get to Q, there must be a state P1 that is an arrival state of S1 and a starting state for S2.

Thus, the establishment of proof is based on an inference process that allows obtaining a proof tree. For example, we put the tree of proof (Figure 11.18) associated with a piece of program that contains a loop "until".

$$\{P\}\ S1\ \{P1\}\qquad \{P1\}S2\{Q\}$$

$$\overline{\qquad\qquad\qquad\qquad\qquad\qquad\qquad}$$

$$\{P\}\ S1\ ;\ S2\ \{Q\}$$

Figure 11.17. *Sequent of the sequence*

$$[I\ \&e = true]\ C\ [I]\qquad\qquad [I\ \&\ e=false]\ =>Q$$

$$\overline{\qquad\qquad\qquad\qquad\qquad\qquad\qquad\qquad\qquad}$$

P & C0   [I] While e do C [Q]

$$\overline{\qquad\qquad\qquad\qquad\qquad\qquad\qquad\qquad\qquad}$$

[P] C0 ; While e do C [Q]

Figure 11.18. *Tree of proof*

Tools for support in demonstration have been developed. They are of three categories:

– *Interactive proof tools*: they are an aid to the management of the demonstration;

– *Automatic proof tools*: they are capable of performing, from a base of mathematical rules, the proof of a theorem;

– *Verification tools of the proof*: they are capable, from a tree of proof, to verify the correction of the demonstration that was carried out.

11.3.1.3.14. Formal method

Formal methods [MON 00] are based on the use of discrete mathematics to prove that programs verify properties. In [OFT 97], there is a presentation of examples of use of different formal methods by the manufacturers. Formal methods regroup languages whose semantics is defined mathematically and techniques of transformation and verification are based on mathematical proof.

These methods include petri networks, method B [ABR 96], SCADE [DOR 08], VDM [JON 90] and Z [SPI 89]. As an example of implementation, we will present the example of the system SAET_METEOR. Line 14 of the Paris metro, named METEOR [CHA 96], is managed by SAET, which is a complex distributed real time whose main function is to ensure the transport of travellers, while ensuring a very high safety level for the travellers.

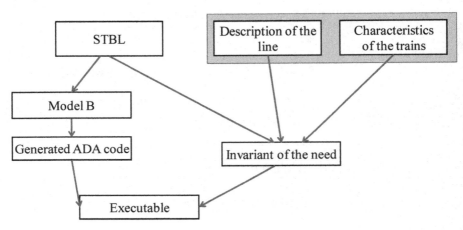

Figure 11.19. *Formal development process of a parameterized application*

The separation between the data and the code (Figure 11.19) above all allows eliminating errors of compatibility between equipment, but it especially allows obtaining a generic description of the equipment.

From the description of the software needs of equipment, it is possible to build a model B and to define a set of data called need invariants that are derived from the topological invariants. Need invariants are associated with particular equipment.

Figure 11.20 shows an example of a development process for a formal application. This process is the one that has been implemented in the context of the use of method B [ABR 96] in the framework of development ([BEH 96] and [BOU 06, Chapter 3]) of SAET-METEOR.

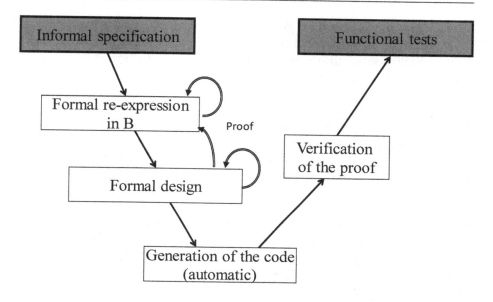

Figure 11.20. *Development process of a formal application*

The translation of model B [ABR 96] into the language ADA [ANS 83, ISO 95, BAR 14] is safe and automatically performed by the tool. The safety aspect is obtained through the subset of the code ADA and through the use of the safe code processor (PSC, see [BOU 10, Chapter 2]), which ensures the safety of the execution.

The presence of the formal proof of compliance of the code developed compared to the specifications allowed to significantly reduce the phases of the cycle test V, which is schematized in Figure 11.20.

The implementation of method B [ABR 96, BOU 14a] on the SAET-METEOR (see [BOU 06, Chapter 3]) helped to demonstrate that it was possible to replace testing activities (TU and TI) by evidence activities.

But without raising controversy on the use of formal methods in the context of safety software [BEH 96], it is said that the unit tests and integration tests are redundant with full proof and safe code generation.

Waeselynck and Jean-Louis [WAE 95] advocate preserving all test phases; in expectation of returning on the methodology and validation of tools B, this discussion is still valid if the development is performed in a context out of coded safety processor (architecture CSP).

It should be noted that realizing and validating a model B does not guarantee that the code generator, executable production tools (compiler, linker, etc.), installation tools, configuration management tools and target hardware architecture do not transform the execution and therefore make the evidence that has been made obsolete.

In the context of Figure 11.18, we have introduced the generic software concept parameterized by the data. This practice is very common in the context of rail and/or automotive applications. In the framework of [BOU 03, BOU 07], we have shown that it was possible to implement formal techniques for the verification and the validation of the compliance of data associated with a rail application.

Data-related properties may be properties of safety (safety) or other; they are introduced into the verification tool through a formal, set language. This set language allows expressing the properties with the classical mathematical operators ($\forall, \exists, \in, \subseteq, \Rightarrow, \Leftrightarrow, \wedge, \neg, \vee$, etc.). The verification of a constraint is performed by exploration of the space of possibilities (topological data), which is equivalent to a proof by case. The constraint verification tool made in the context of the application SAET-METEOR is based on an algorithm similar to model checking.

This verification tool (see [DEL 99]) allows to formally verify data; to date there are more than 100 safety rules that are verified. For example, here are some properties of safety data:

– *P3*: The whole track circuits form a partition of the track (the track connection);

– *P4*: A needle is associated with more than two routes.

11.3.2. *Dynamic verification*

Dynamic verification is based on the partial or total execution of the system.

DEFINITION 11.9.– (DYNAMIC ANALYSIS) [ISO 85]. *Software tool is analyzing the behavior of a program by monitoring its execution.*

A dynamic analyzer allows finding the travelled paths, execution times, resource consumptions, etc.

11.3.2.1. *Analysis of execution*

There are several types of analyses:

– efficiency in the use of resources (execution time, mastering of memory, task management, process management, etc.);

– memory management (allocation/dellocation) to control leaks and misuses;

– test coverage.

11.3.2.2. *Test*

The test [MYE 79, XAN 99] is a dynamic verification technique that consists of running the system (or one of its components) by providing it with entry values.

DEFINITION 11.10.– (TESTING A SOFTWARE APPLICATION) [MYE 79]. Testing is executing the program with the intention of finding anomalies or defects.

The test and the development of a program are two separate activities, but are closely related:

– the test can reveal the existence of defects in a program and verify that the development has corrected them properly and has not generated new ones;

– the development begins when a defect is identified. It allows locating it in the program to design the correction and carry it out.

The development cycle is divided into phases, and the test takes place in several of these stages. As shown in Figure 11.21, there are unit tests, integration tests and functional validation tests.

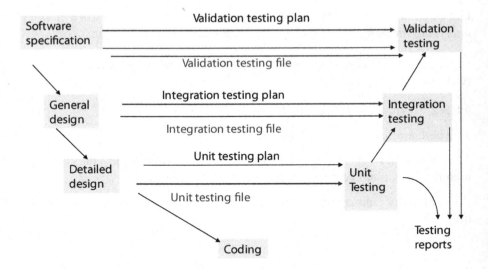

Figure 11.21. *The different test campaigns*

The activities (see Figure 11.22) linked to the tests can be divided into the following:

– selection of test sets;

– submission;

– stripping (must use an oracle);

– evaluation.

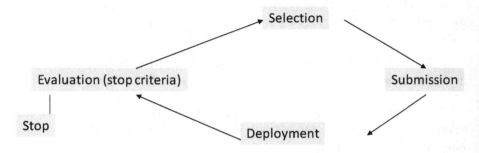

Figure 11.22. *Activities linked to tests*

There are a few questions as follows:

– how to choose the program entries?

– how to decide that the result is good or bad (oracle problem)?

– when to do the tests?

– which tools?

– when to stop the tests (test coverage measurement problem)?

Volume 4 of this collection [BOU 17b] will be dedicated to the presentation of test strategies. All sections 11.3.2.2 allow introduction of the general concepts in order to present the test as a V&V technique of a software application.

11.3.2.2.1. Selection of test cases

The selection of test cases is the primary activity and is often manual, but in certain cases may be equipped.

Following the test steps, the repository can be very different in nature:

– UT: we have the sources. An analysis of the sources allows choosing the best tests to undertake. We talk about white box testing;

– IT: there is a description of the software architecture and a description of the interactions between the hardware and software;

– VT or OST: there are only specifications. The tests are therefore called black box.

Concerning the phases of IT and VT, there are two types of activities:

– manual selection of test cases: in the absence of a model, the tester must build his/her test catalogue through his/her knowledge;

– selection by exploration: it is possible to achieve a model of specifications and an exploration of this model allows choosing the test cases.

11.3.2.2.2. Execution of the test cases

The UT and IT software/software are generally performed on the development machine. They consist of the realization of a specific program written in the language of the application. For these test families, it is important to be able to replay the test identically, both to demonstrate the correction and to manage the evolutions (induced by the correction of anomalies). There are test environments that, from a description of the test case (inputs to provide and intended outputs), is able to carry out all of the executions, archiving of the results, results analysis and the production of a balance sheet test folder.

For the VT or OST, they may be performed either on a "host" machine or on a "target" machine. They require the establishment of specific environments that are generally dedicated to the project. These environments must allow simulating the environment in a more or less realistic way.

11.3.2.2.3. Stripping of tests

The stripping of tests is an essential phase that aims to verify that the results obtained are consistent with the expected results. The stripping of the test results can be performed manually or automatically.

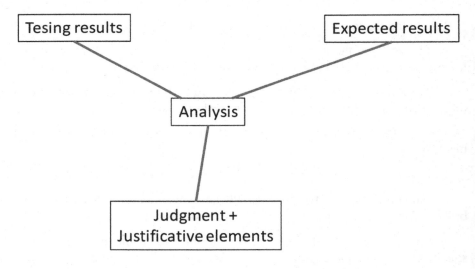

Figure 11.23. *Stripping phase*

11.3.2.2.4. Coverage measure

One of the important questions for the project is "how to decide the ending of tests?"; there are several possible answers:

– sufficient confidence has been reached (purely subjective);

– aim of instructions coverage has been reached;

– structural coverage has been reached;

– aim of input and output coverage has been reached;

– coverage has been reached;

– the number of estimated residual errors is acceptable;

– and finally, there is no more budget.

The concept of coverage level implies the possibility of having information on the execution path associated with each test. This information can be obtained through two mechanisms:

– an instrumentation of code, therefore there is modification of the source code. This modification can impact the behavior of the application (at least from the temporal point of view). This type of instrumentation is realized when working on the "host" equipment;

– a physical instrumentation on processor level (probe), bus level, etc. This type of instrumentation is realized when working on the "target" equipment.

11.3.3. *Validation*

Validation is normally performed on the final product. Validation is based on validation tests that are performed on the final equipment (target). The issue of the tests has been discussed in section 11.3.2.2 and will be detailed in Volume 4 [BOU 17b].

11.4. Verification and validation plan

According to the lifecycle implemented on the project (in general the V cycle, see Figure 11.1), safety level to achieve and the V&V process chosen on the project, it is necessary to describe the methodology within a software verification and validation plan (SVVP).

The SVVP should describe:

– the organization;

– the means: who, what tools, etc.;

– the methods;

– the elements handled: lists of elements in entries, identification of elements produced and lists of documents to produce;

– the objective: coverage percentage, verification objective, milestone planning, etc.

11.5. New issues of the V&V

This chapter was an opportunity to rapidly present all the techniques applicable in the context of the V&V activities, namely reviews (code review, document review, etc.), the static analysis of code (qualimetry, abstract interpretation, verification of coding rules, etc.), the dynamic analysis of code (unit tests, integration tests, validation tests, etc.), etc.

As discussed in the introduction (see section 1.1), the standards applicable to the various areas (Aeronautical [RTA 92, RTA 11], Automotive [ISO 11], Rail [CEN 01, CEN 11, IEC 14], Nuclear [IEC 06] and Generic [IEC 08]) recommend the establishment of a quality insurance (Chapter 2) based on the establishment of a development cycle of type "V cycle" (see Figure 11.3).

It is worth noting that these different standards define the notion of "safety level to achieve" (DAL in aeronautics, SIL for the generic standard, SSIL for rail, ASIL for automobile). The safety level is generally linked to an effort to implement; this effort can be linked to an objective to achieve (aeronautics) or means to implement (automobile, railway, generic domains).

For example, Table 11.7 presents the realization phase of a *software requirements specification*. It is extracted from the standard CENELEC EN 50128 [CEN 01, CEN11]. It is worth noting that the *software requirements specification* always requires a description of the problem in natural language and all the necessary mathematical notations to reflect the application. It is worth noting that for the rail domain, similar tables appear for the architecture and design phase.

	SSIL0	SSIL1	SSIL2	SSIL3	SSIL4
Formal methods including, for example, CCS, CSP, HOL, LOTOS, OBJ, temporal logic, VDM, Z and B	–	R	R	HR	HR
Semiformal methods	R	R	R	HR	HR
Structured method including, for example, JSD, MASCOT, SADT, SDL, SSADM and Yourdon	R	HR	HR	HR	HR

Table 11.7. *CENELEC EN 50128 – Table A.2*

Under the standards of the areas of Automobile [ISO 11], Railway [CEN 01, CEN 11, IEC 14] and Generic [IEC 08], the formal methods are recommended (see Table 1.1) as a means to capture the needs and lead to the production of a mastered code.

Formal methods such as method B [ABR 96, BOU 14a] or SCADE[5] [DOR 08] allow acquiring a need, to formalize it in the form of a model, to demonstrate the respect of the properties and to produce a code that is the image of the model.

If the tools implemented (simulator, proover, code generator, etc.) are demonstrated with respect to the objectives related to the safety level to achieve by the application, this type of approach allows replacing the activities of V&V by other activities (for example unit tests can be replaced by a qualification/certification of the code generator, see [BOU 06]).

Standards therefore take into account the use of formal techniques when they are associated with models (see sections 11.3.1.2.10, 11.3.1.3.11 and 11.3.1.3.12), which are associated with documents of design (specification, architecture and conception).

---

5 SCADE is distributed by the company Esterel-Technologies. See the website http://www. esterel-technologies.com.

Currently, the coding phase is based on the use of a programming language such ADA [ANS 83, ISO 95, BAR 14], C [ISO 99] and/or C++. Originally, these languages were not related to formal techniques of verification.

As we shall see in the following chapters, it may be quite difficult to achieve the activities of V&V such as the final code's review and tests (of type ADA, C or C++) and it may be interesting to implement formal techniques such as abstract interpretation [COU 00] and/or the evidence (of evidence type HOARE [HOA 69]) that will allow identifying the properties respected by the code and/or demonstrate that the code verifies certain properties.

11.6. Conclusion

The development of a certifiable software application is constrained by the requirements of the standards associated with each domain (Aeronautical [RTA 92, RTA 11], Automobile [ISO 11], Railway [CEN 01, CEN 11, IEC 14], Nuclear [IEC 06], Generic [IEC 08]). These prescriptive requirements recommend the implementation of a development process of type "V cycle", which is based on V&V activities based on the realization of the test (UT, IT, VT and OST).

The implementation of test activities suffers from several problems, which are as follows:

– the cost and heaviness of testing activities;

– the late detection of defects;

– the difficulty to perform all tests.

Therefore, it is necessary to implement other practices that must allow detecting as soon as possible and in a broader way the defects of the software application.

The establishment of an equipped V&V will require qualification of associated tools; these will be classified as T2[6]. The qualification process has been presented in Chapter 13.

One of the possible orientations is to implement formal methods (for example method B [ABR 96, BOU 14a], SCADE [DOR 08], VDM [JON 90], Z [SPI 89], etc.), which on the basis of a model and a set of properties allow demonstrating that the software produced verifies the said properties.

But it can be interesting, based on the classical development languages (like C), to explore the program behaviors and demonstrate that it checks a number of properties. The demonstration is only possible through the adding of annotations describing local conditions (precondition, postcondition, invariant) and a mechanism of propagation and/or of evidence.

In Volumes 3 and 4 [BOU 17a, BOU 17b], we will present examples of implementation of static analysis techniques of code based on abstract interpretation [COU 00, BOU 11] and proof of program [HOA 69].

It is worth noting that one of the difficulties in the implementation of these techniques resides in their lack of recognition within current standards. Indeed, certain standards (CENELEC EN 50128 [CEN 01, CEN 11] for example) advocate the implementation of formal methods, but do not mention the concept of abstract interpretation (or derived methods).

---

6 Class T2 is dedicated to tools where a defect may distort the results of verification or validation. Class T2 contains the tools of verification of coding standards, metrics measurement, static analysis of code, management and execution of tests, etc.

Tools Management

12.1. Introduction

As shown in Figure 12.1, the realization of software applications requires the use of tools such as model editing tools and/or code testing tools, analysis tools, configuration management tools, etc.

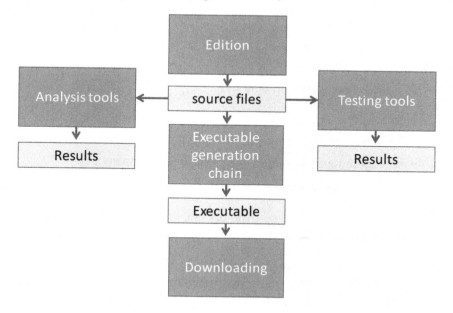

Figure 12.1. *Example of tool processes*

Thus, to ensure the maintainability of a software application, it is necessary:

– to have a complete list of tools used for the software realization;

– to have a precise description of the machinery required for each step of the realization cycle (computer dedicated to testing are usually different from the computer dedicated to producing the executable);

– to have a description of the executable generation process;

– to manage the complete configuration (documents, file, tools, etc.).

Within the following sections, we will present in more detail the needs and associated issues.

12.2. List of tools

The first essential document about the tools is the tool list. To ensure the maintenance of a software application, it is necessary to have a set of tools that allows for the realization of an application, the tool list the contains:

– the name;

– the useable functions (and options);

– the reference;

– the version;

– the type: commercial or developed within the company;

– a specification or a technical manual.

The list of tools may be a specific document but it can also be dispersed among the various project documents.

Within a company or within a project, it is necessary to show that the set of tools forms a coherent whole. The coherent whole means that we must demonstrate that the transition from one tool to another limits defects.

Indeed, if it is necessary to introduce a tool that aims to change the format or changing from one concept to another (for example a functional approach to object-oriented approach), we run the risk of introducing defects.

12.3. Description of the computer

Tools are a delicate part of the software realization process and their implementation is directly related to computers. It is therefore necessary to identify the type of computer (processor, memory, etc.) and the operating system (OS).

Even though on previous projects (e.g. for the SACEM developed in the 1980s), it was possible to keep old computers, due to recent IT developments, it is necessary to work with more up to date machines.

One of the best ways to handle this problem is to implement a virtualization of the execution computer; it will thus be possible to work with this virtual machine instead of a real computer. This solution involves the establishment of a virtual machine early in the project (avoid waiting for the project to be finalized).

The implementation of virtualization requires the ability to guarantee the capacity to run this virtual machine to allow a follow-up of the versions throughout and after the project.

12.4. Generation process

The management of tools has a direct impact on the maintainability of a software application. But different tools do not have different same impact and they can be classified into different families:

– editing tools (model, text, code, etc.);

– data generation tools;

– compilation tools;

– static analysis tools (metric programming rules, abstract interpretation, etc.);

– testing tools;

– configuration management tools.

Among these, one subset of tools are more important that the others. Effectively, the tools involved in the executable generation process have a greater impact on the final product. A defect during the generation process can introduce a defect in the executable. We are referring to the executable generation process. In Figure 12.2, an example of the executable generation process is shown.

It is necessary to formalize this process and verify that all of the tools are identified, as no stage should be forgotten. The formalization of the executable generation process can be done in a specific document or in the software version sheet.

The executable generation process must be tested to see if it can generate a unique executable. We avoid using tools that introduce dates. For example, compilers such as Visual-C add compilation dates in the executable.

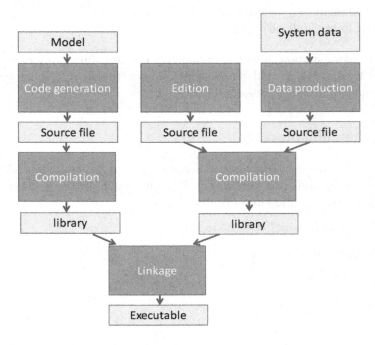

Figure 12.2. *Generation process*

Another difficulty with compilers is related to the notion of static and dynamic software. In modern OS, it is very difficult to produce a static executable; we need to use a specific library done by the compiler, the COTS and/or the OS.

This executable generation process should be subject to a safety study to identify the mitigations to be implemented in order to control the potential risk induced by the tools.

In certain fields, such as in the railway industry, it happens that the customer requires reinstallation of the development environment on a new machine and the implementation of the executable generation process in order to ensure that the generation of the executable has been delivered. For example, if a customer installs tools and then updates these after some time, it is not possible to identify the version and the tools seller explain that the only way to have the same executable is done by a physical copy of the file from the initial computer to the new computer.

12.5. Tool configuration management

For commercial tools, configuration management is needed to save the supplied elements (CD, executable, documentation, license server, license, etc.). It will also be necessary to develop ways to ensure availability of this tool and licenses for a given period.

For an internally developed tool, we check that its realization process conforms to at least the ISO 9001:2015 standard that identifies the need for a development and maintenance process, specification, validation and version sheet. In general, internally developed tools have no documentation, the code does not respect programming rules, the language used for development has bad properties (for example Perl, Python and C#), no tests and no verification exist and it is very difficult to maintain.

12.6. Tool qualification

Initially, the development of a software application involved producing a code. The obtaining of an executable then goes through the use of a compiler. If the process to get the code conforms to a safety objective (ASIL, DAL, SSIL, etc.), the fact that the software application is consistent with its safety objective is directly related to the compiler. It must be demonstrated that the compiler is used for a given safety objective, where we speak of tool qualification.

More generally, this problem can be generalized to all tools used for design, compilation, verification and validation of the software application, and also for the tools used in data production of the software application. For these tools, it is then asked to set up a qualification.

At the system level, there are two types of tools: (i) measuring tools (oscilloscope, multimeter, etc.) for which it is necessary to respect the rules of calibration and benchmarking and (ii) software tools. For software tools such as tools related to configuration management, implementation of equipment, implementation of equipment testing, equipment, subsystems and system, etc., we must go through the setting up of a qualification. This qualification is designed to demonstrate that the tool is appropriate in the context of a particular project.

Also, in the context of software application realization, a number of tools are implemented such as editors, compilers, linkers, configuration management tools, download tools, test environments, simulators, etc.

The qualification effort of a tool is to be associated with risks induced by the tool on the final product. These tools can thus be classified into three families:

– F1: tools that impact the executable generation process;

– F2: tools that impact the verification;

– F3: tools that have no impact on the generation of the final executable and the verification.

The F1 family requires that one is able to demonstrate, in the context of the use that is made for the application in progress, that no fault can be introduced into the final application. The F2 family requires demonstrating that the existing defects cannot undermine the results of the verification. F2 Family tools must not allow indicating that verification is OK if it is KO.

The DO 178 standard version B already introduced the notion of tool qualification and this idea was included in the IEC 61508 version 2008, and therefore in derived standards such as ISO 26262 and CENELEC EN 50128 standard in 2011 version.

The purpose of Chapter 13 is to present the principles of the qualification of the tools used in the context of the realization of a critical and reliable software application that will be submitted for certification.

12.7. Conclusion

This chapter has introduced several needs like the list of tools, computers management and the definition of a process for the generation of the executable. It may seem that these are obvious considerations that are normally taken into account by the projects. But this is not the case in many projects and it is when making a change that we discover the existence of tools that have not been put in configuration or whose documentation is minimal.

13

Tools Qualification

13.1. Introduction

In the framework of software application realization, a large number of tools such as editors, compilers, linkers, configuration management tools, download tools, test environments, simulators, etc., are implemented.

As we have indicated, it is necessary to have a list of all the tools used on the project and manage the impact of the tools on the final product. To do this, we will discuss the qualification of the tools. Thus, the effort of tool qualification is to associate the risks induced by tools on the final product. These tools can be grouped into the following three families:

– F1: tools having an impact on the generation of the executable;

– F2: tools having an impact on the verification and validation;

– F3: tools not having any impact on the generation of the final executable nor on the verification and validation.

The purpose of this chapter is to present the principles of the management of the tools used in the realization of a safety critical software application, which will be subject to a certification objective.

The first objective is to have a complete list of the tools used during software application realization. In general, during maintenance, we find that only some tools are needed and these are not managed properly (licenses for test, many versions are used, version is not known because it is applied to many patches, internal tools have no source file, etc.).

13.2. Tools qualification

13.2.1. *Presentation*

Very often the choice of the tools used for the realization of a software application is not formalized, while they may have a direct impact on the final executable.

As we have explained, it must be demonstrated that a tool can be used as part of the realization of a software application with a determined safety goal. This activity is called tool qualification (see definition below).

DEFINITION 13.1 (Tool Qualification).– *Tool qualification is a process that allows us to demonstrate that a tool can be used as part of the realization of a software application with a determined safety goal.*

In the following sections, we will present in a more precise manner what qualification is by clarifying the inputs, outputs and activities.

13.2.2. *Standards synthesis*

The objective of this section is to provide an overview of the needs that are outlined within the different standards concerning tool qualification.

13.2.2.1. *DO 178*

As we stated in Volume 1 [BOU 16], the DO 178 standard is dedicated to the realization of software applications in the aeronautical field. This standard in its B version is the first to introduce the concept of tools qualification.

13.2.2.1.1. Version B

In the B version, the DO 178 [ARI 92] standard addresses the need to set up a qualification of the tools (see section 12.2). The DO 178 standard makes the qualification of tools necessary if the process identified in the standard is affected (withdrawal or reduction of activity, automation, etc.) through the use of a tool.

The DO 178 standard in B version introduces two families of tools:

– software development tools: outputs are integrated to the embedded software application;

– audit tools of the software: these tools do not introduce errors but may be unable to detect errors.

The DO 178 standard in the B version indicates that the qualification is valid for use on a particular system; therefore, there is no capitalization.

The qualification process is therefore to:

– identify the type of tool: development tools (CC1) or audit tools (CC2);

– identify the tool's level: tool's software level must be the same as that of the embedded software application unless we can justify a reduction of the level. The reduction of the level is linked to the type of activity affected, the importance of the affected activity, the probability of detecting an anomaly by some other means, etc.;

– implement a quality assurance process similar to that   should be implemented for an embedded application;

– check the specification of the tool and ensure it meets them: section 12.2.1 of the DO 178 describes the activities to be implemented;

– validate the performance of the tool. It is possible to put the tool under supervision during a certain period in order to confirm that the outputs are correct.

– manage defects: all the tool's defects must be registered, analyzed and corrected;

– put in place a configuration management process similar to that should be put in place for an embedded application.

The qualification process, described above, should give rise to records.

For each tool, a qualification plan needs to be written in order to identify the tool's configuration, the level looked for (CC1 or CC2), the level required (design assurance level), a description of the architecture, an identification of the activities to be realized and an identification of the data to be produced. Please note that the certification authority gives qualification approval.

13.2.2.1.2. Version C

In version C of the DO 178 [RTA 11a] standard, several fascicles have been introduced including a fascicle dedicated to the qualification of tools, which is named DO 330 [RTA 11b]. The DO 330 guide summarizes the categories CC1 and CC2 and introduces a qualification objective named Tool Qualification Level (TQL), which goes from 1 to 5.

The DO 330 guide proposes a radical philosophy change compared to version B of the DO 178 standard and other standards (IEC 61508, ISO 26262, 50128). Indeed, it is proposed to put in place a realization process of the tools, which is not the DO 178 standard but a specific process and lightened compared to the standard demands of the field. This approach is innovative and more realistic.

13.2.2.2. IEC 61508

In its 2008 version, the IEC 61508 [IEC 08] standard identifies three tool classes: T1, T2 and T3. The three classes are defined as follows:

– T1: generates no output and does not contribute, directly or indirectly, to the executable code (including data) of the safety-related system.

– T2: supports the test or the verification of the conception or the executable code when tool-specific errors may prevent the detection of errors but cannot directly create errors in the executable software.

– T3: generates outputs that may contribute, directly or indirectly, to the executable code of the safety-related system.

From these classes, the IEC 61508:2008 standard identifies the need to set up a qualification process.

13.2.2.3. *ISO 26262*

In its 2011 version, the ISO 26262 standard also identifies three classes for the tools named tool confidence level (TCL). As shown in Table 13.1, which is extracted from Part 8 of the ISO 26262 standard, it is necessary to identify the impact of a failure of the tool (TI) and the detection capacity of the error (TD).

0		Tool error detection (TD)		
		TD1	TD2	TD3
Tool Impact (TI)	TI1	TCL1	TCL1	TCL1
	TI2	TCL1	TCL2	TCL3

Table 13.1. *Table of the ISO 26262 standard concerning the TCL*

TCL2 and TCL3 are the two classes that require the establishment of a set of actions that are to be selected (see, for example, Table 13.2 for a TCL3) taking into account the automotive safety integrity level (ASIL) of the software.

	Methods	ASIL			
		A	B	C	D
a	Increase of trust through usage	++	++	+	+
b	Assessment of the development process of the tool	++	++	+	+
c	Validation of the tool	+	+	++	++
d	Developed in compliance with trade standards	+	+	++	++

Table 13.2. *The ISO 26262 standard concerning the management of the TCL3*

Tools qualification may be realized as the combination of four activities:

– return of experience;

– evaluation of the tool's realization process;

– implementation of the tool's validation;

– tool's realization in accordance with the trade standards: ISO 26262, DO 178 or IEC 61508.

13.2.2.4. *CENELEC EN 50128*

The CENELEC EN 50128 [CEN 01, CEN 11] standard is dedicated to the realization of software applications for the railway field. Note that the CENELEC standard is applicable at the European level and the IEC 62279 [IEC 14] is the applicable version at the international level. The CENELEC 50128 and IEC 62279 standards are equivalent with respect to the qualification of tools.

13.2.2.4.1. 2001 version

Under section 10.4.7 (conception section), the CENELEC EN 50128:2001 standard requires a suitable set of tools to be chosen (conception methods, language, compiler) for the software safety integrity level (SSIL) and the whole of the software's lifecycle.

More precisely, section 10.4.9 introduces a request concerning the language selection; the compiler had to have one of the following elements:

– a validation certificate;

– an evaluation report;

– a redundant process;

– a process to reduce the impact of the tools on the final product.

Some languages such as ADA (see, for example, [ANS 83, ISO 95]) have a standard describing the language, and it is possible to put in place a certification process. For example, in the context of the certification of ADA compilers, the existence of a standard and a quite fine semantic of the ADA language allows us to define a certification process of a compiler. This process has been implemented on different compilers. This process is based on a sequence of tests named ADA Conformity Assessment Test Suite (ACATS) (see the [ADA 01] standard). For more information on ACATS, see [ADA 99]. This approach, although applicable, remains confidential.

The second possibility is to carry out an evaluation report, which details the merits of the compiler usage in this context. This approach is what we call compiler qualification.

For the third case, the standard was more precise because it indicated "a redundant process based on a signature control that allows for detecting translation errors". This approach is directly inherited from a coded safety processor (CSP) used in French railways ([BOU 09], Chapter 2]). The CSP has been implemented in the context of the SACEM (aid system for conduct, exploitation and maintenance) and deployed on multiple similar systems. The CSP is based on a redundant process that produces an executable and a series of codes, and on hardware architecture capable of running the application while achieving a verification of the predetermined offline codes during execution. Although interesting, this type of redundancy is very specific and not used very much.

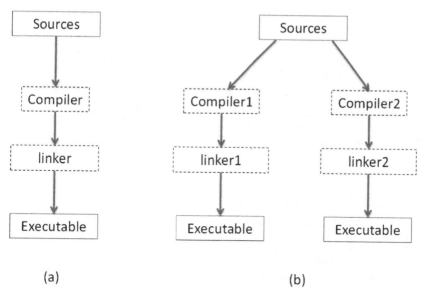

Figure 13.1. Two examples of a compilation chain

There is a last case; it is, indeed, possible to implement a generation process of the executable that is based, for example, on two channels (see Figure 13.1) or which introduces verification activities that are manual for example.

Measure	SSIL0	SSIL1 SSIL2	SSIL3 SSIL4
...			
11. Validated translator	R	HR	HR
12. Translator proven at use	HR	HR	HR
...			

Table 13.3. *Table A.4 of the EN 50128:2001 standard*

As shown in Table 13.3, as part of the conception, we focus on the translator (in the compiler sense) with a link to the B.7 section passing as a validated translator to certified compiler with a generalization to all the tools.

Note that line 12 concerning the translator proven at use is related to section B.65 that identifies the concept of compiler proven at use. This concept allows enhancing the acquired experience for a given version of a compiler. This experience needs to be formalized and should identify projects (nature, complexity, safety level, etc.) and the known anomalies. This approach has a downside of limiting the introduction of new languages and/or new compilers.

We can conclude that under the CENELEC EN 50128:2001 standard, there was a request for the qualification of compilers, without really indicating what was expected.

13.2.2.4.2. 2011 version

The 2011 version of the CENELEC EN 50128 standard formally introduces the need of qualifying tools (see section 6.7 of the standard). As for the IEC 61508 and the ISO 26262 standards, three classes of tools have been introduced: T1, T2, T3. The three classes are defined as follows:

– *T1*: It generates no output like to contribute, directly or indirectly, to the executable code (including data) of the software.

– *T2*: It allows the test or verification of the conception or executable code, while internal errors to the tool may not be able to reveal defects but without directly creating errors in the executable software.

– *T3*: It generates outputs that may contribute, directly or indirectly, to the executable code (including data) of the safety-related system.

The definition of T2 is the same as for the IEC 61508:2008 standard. For T1, we focalize on the software and for T3 we add the data.

In the end, the T1 class is dedicated to tools that have no impact on the audit and have no impact on the final executable, being:

– editing tools (text editor, model editor, etc.) without the ability to generate elements to integrate in the code;

– auxiliary tools such as configuration management tools.

The T2 class is dedicated to tools where a defect could distort the verification or validation results. The T2 class contains the verification tools of coding standards, metrics measurement, static code analysis, management and execution of tests, coverage measurement tools, etc.

The T3 class is dedicated to tools whose failure could have an effect of the final executable. This class includes compilers, code generators, data preparation tools, etc.

13.3. Qualification process

In all of the current standards, we see the need to qualify the tools in regard to their usage. To do this, we take the family classification, which has been presented in the introduction and for each family, a qualification strategy must be set.

The qualification notion is an important concept that is related to the implementation of tools in the realization process of a software application. All the tools used may be subject to a qualification phase.

Regarding the qualification, we have chosen to follow in part the approach of the CENELEC EN 50128:2011 [CEN 11] standard but we will complete with the requirements of other standards.

13.3.1. *Qualification report*

The different standards (DO 178, ISO 26262, and CENELEC EN 50128) are or will bring up the notion of a "qualification report". The standards, and in particular section 6.7 of the CENELEC EN 50128:2011 standard, define for each class of tools a set of recommendations that allow us to identify the contents of the qualification report (that we will call tools qualification report).

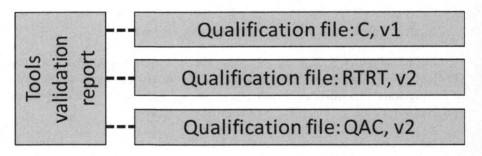

Figure 13.2. *Tools' validation file versus qualification report*

The qualification report can rely on different types of activities:

– analysis of the use of a certificate (we speak of cross-acceptance): if a certificate exists, please verify that the tool is suitable for the intended use (the same normative referential, similar safety level, etc.);

– construction of a return of experience: it consists of a census of all uses (those of the company and those known). It is necessary at this moment to be able to justify the used versions, safety levels, size, fields, etc.;

– establishment of a qualification: a series of tests of the tool can be performed to demonstrate that the tool is suitable for a given safety level.

The CENELEC EN 50128:2011 standard proposes to carry out a global document named "validation report" of the tools. This validation report should thus cover all the tools of the project. In the case of an industrial project, it is better to build independent reports which are managed at the tool-team level rather than by the project team. The validation reports of the tools at the project level are then (see Figure 13.2) used to reference the qualification reports (reference and version).

13.3.2. Qualification process

The CENELEC EN 50128:2011 standard identifies 12 requirements (from 6.7.4.1 to 6.7.4.12) concerning tools qualification. The 6.7.4.12 requirement is presented in Table 13.4, which has been corrected from the published version. In this table, we have mentioned the steps that allow us to classify the requirements to be implemented. The steps will be explained in the following section.

Class of tools	Applicable paragraphs	Step
T1	6.7.4.1	Identification
T2	6.7.4.1	Identification
	6.7.4.2	Justification
	6.7.4.3	Specification
	6.7.4.10, 6.7.4.11	Version management
T3	6.7.4.1	Identification
	6.7.4.2	Justification
	6.7.4.3	Specification
	(6.7.4.4 and 6.7.4.5 or 6.7.4.6)	Evidence of compliance
	(6.7.4.7 or 6.7.4.8) and 6.7.4.9	Adequacy to the needs
	6.7.4.10, 6.7.4.11	Version management

Table 13.4. *Table 1 of the CENELEC EN 50128:2001 standard*

Table 13.4 presents an increase in efforts to be implemented but is incomplete because it does not take into account the level of the SSIL. The

IEC 62279:2014 [IEC 14] standard is the image of the CENELEC EN 50128 standard. The version being finalized of IEC 62279:2014 standard is presented in Table 13.5.

From Table 13.4, we can identify a methodology for the qualification of the tools that is divided into five activities:

– *identification*: necessary to identify the tool and the version used;

– *justification*: necessary to identify and justify the Tx class of the tool;

– *evidence of compliance*: the tool must have a specification and is necessary to show that the tool meets this specification;

– *adequacy to the needs*: necessary to show that the tool is in adequacy with the global methodology of the software development;

– *version management*: necessary to manage in configuration the qualified version and to control the known anomalies.

Class of tools	Methodology	SSIL
T1	None	–
T2 T3	Successful usage demonstration in similar environments	1–2
	Support process implemented in addition to the tool	
	Execution of a library of test cases showing the correct operation of the tool	
	Compliance with all of the requirements of the 50128 for the development of the tool	3–4
	Justification for the existence of an implementation process of the tool allowing to demonstrate the level of the SSIL	
	Execution of a library of recognized test cases showing the correct operation of the tool	
	Execution of a process using several different tools with a process of comparison	

Table 13.5. *Table 3 of the IEC 62279 standard*

The IEC 62279:2014 [IEC 14] standard introduces for each 6.7.4.x item complimentary precisions that do not change the base of the requirements of the CENELEC EN 50128:2011 standard.

13.3.3. *Implementation of the qualification process*

13.3.3.1. *Identification*

This first activity is quite simple, in the sense that it consists of identifying the tool to be used (name, reference, functions, etc.) and to explain why this tool is necessary.

During the process definition, we need to identify all tools used in the different activities. Indeed, it is necessary to explain the merits of implementing the tool, its adequacy to the safety objectives and the functions that are used or that are usable.

In the 2001 version of the CENELEC EN 50128 standard, there already was a request to show that the conception process was adequate with the objectives of the SSIL. In the 2011 version, we are asked to go further and to think about the entire process and therefore the cooperation between tools, the compatibility of files and formats, the idea being to minimize the number of errors (coming from tools, exchanges and handling).

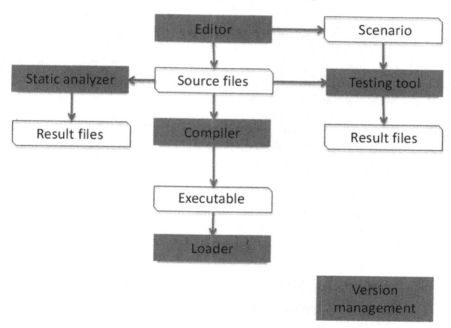

Figure 13.3. *Tools in the process*

The tools are of different natures: specification tools, modeling tools, code generators, compilers, loaders, test environments, configuration management tools, etc.

Figure 13.3 shows an example of an equipped process that allows the appearing of the editing tools, the executable generating tools, verification and validation tools and configuration management tools.

Function	Level 1	Client	Target
Configure	Define a configuration	X	
	Send a configuration	X	X
	Simulate equipment		X
Simulate	Reading/writing	X	X
Edit a scenario	Add a scenario	X	
	Modify a scenario	X	
	Remove a scenario	X	

Table 13.6. *Example of the identification of tool features*

One of the difficulties of the implementation of the tools lies in the number of features they offer. We should then be able to define the functional perimeter to qualify (see Table 13.6). It is generally difficult to have a complete specification of each tool and the validation effort is then proportional to the number of used features.

From the quality point of view, it is necessary to identify each tool used to perform the software application. To do this, there must be, in the quality referential, a procedure defining the process of selection and management of a tool.

This procedure should rely on the identification of:

– need;

– domain of use;

– involvement level of the tool and the induced safety level;

– possible products (internal or external);

– previous uses;

– requirements (language standards, etc.);

– a qualification policy of the tool regarding the need.

NOTE.– Some compilers can generate different executables (taking account of the date and time, random optimization algorithm: branch selection, etc.).

13.3.3.2. *Justification of the class*

On the basis of the information in the identification phase, it is necessary to identify the impact of a tool failure and therefore the Tx class associated with each tool.

13.3.3.2.1. Choice of the Tx

For each tool, we should, starting from its role in the realization process of the software application, identify the associated Tx. This step is tricky because some tools may have different roles in different projects.

For example, in project A, a spreadsheet can be used to edit requirements (number, attributes and description); in this context, it will be T1. For project B, the spreadsheet can be used as a tool for visualization and analysis of test results, even as a generator of test results; in this context, the tool will be classified as T2. But for project C, the same tool can be used as a generation means (through the use of macros) of data files in ASCII format, and in this case it will be classified as T3. This example of the spreadsheet shows the difficulty of the qualification and the fact that it is necessary to analyze the use of the tool in the realization process of the software application.

13.3.3.2.2. Analysis of defects

The second step of this phase is to perform a simplified dysfunctional analysis. This is because we do not seek to carry out a safety study of the tool but to identify the impact of a defect of the tool in the overall process. Table 13.7 presents an example of dysfunctional analysis of configured and simulated services that are presented in Table 13.6.

Table 13.8 presents a more complete model plan to achieve a dysfunctional analysis at tool level, but it is only a proposal.

ID	Function	Subfunction	Failure mode	Effect on the conduct of a test	Detection	Risk reduction measure	Comment
1	Configure	Configure a simulation	Establishme nt of a misconfigur ation	Non-executable scenario	Detectable		
				Executed scenario	Detectable		Misconfiguration
				Executed scenario	*Undetectable*	Verification of the configuration before and after the scenarios	T2
2	Simulate	Execution of a simulation	Misinterpret ation of the commands	Non-executable scenario	Detectable		
		Reading of a scenario		Executed scenario	*Undetectable*	Implementati on of tests	T2

Table 13.7. *Example of defect analysis*

ID	Function	Subfunction	Life phase	Defect mode	Effect	Detection	Safety	Risk reduction measure	Comment
1	Fx	SFx	Creation Modification Launching All	No function Degraded function Untimely function Partial function Non-executable function Delayed function	NA Partial element –	Yes No –	nS-S	Tests Verification –	T1 T2 T3 –

Table 13.8. *Dysfunctional analysis type*

13.3.3.2.3. Compiler

In this section, we present a second example of dysfunctional analysis dealing with a compiler. Among the possible defects of a compilation chain, the potentially dangerous situation identified is the production of wrong assembler codes regarding high-level instructions (for example C language) subject of the compilation.

In Table 13.9, we do a simplified analysis of the defects of a compiler and the dangerous situation is then associated with the notion of "degraded function." For this defect, several means of risk reduction are proposed: qualification, double chain, verification of a PSC (see [BOU 10], Chapter 2).

ID	Function	Defect mode	Effect	Detection	Safety	Risk reduction measure	Comment
1		No function	No executable	Yes	nS	–	No performance
		Partial function	No executable	Yes	nS	–	No performance
2	Compiler	Degraded function	Executable	No	S	Validation process	–
						Qualification	T3
						Compilation double chain	–
						Verification of a code against execution errors	Approach type coded processor
						–	
3		Untimely function	No executable	Yes	nS		The generation cannot be achieved without operator control
4		Delayed function	Executable	No	nS	–	No constraint on the compilation time

Table 13.9. *Example of a compiler analysis*

13.3.3.3. *Specification*

As noted earlier, it is necessary to define the functional scope of the classified tools T2 and T3 (see Table 13.6 for example) and to have a specification and/or a user manual that documents used functions. The elements of specification must identify the usage constraints: type of machine, operating system type and version, memory size, usable options, etc.

13.3.3.4. *Evidence of compliance*

As shown in Table 13.4, tool's evidence of compliance is necessary as soon as its class is T3.

13.3.3.4.1. Approach

The CENELEC EN 50128:2011 standard introduces three requirements that must be read as follows ((6.7.4.4 and 6.7.4.5) or 6.7.4.6), unlike what is indicated in Table 1 of the standard.

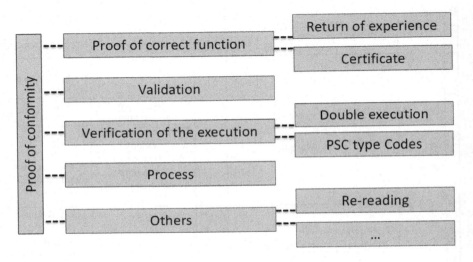

Figure 13.4. *Different approaches for evidence of compliance*

As shown in Figure 13.4, clause 6.7.4.4 identifies the general approach to demonstrate the compliance of the tool and it is based on five approaches: proof of proper functioning (list of previous uses, certificate, etc.), validation, implementation of a verification means of the execution (for example double compilation and comparison and code verification allowing to detect compilation errors), implementation of a process allowing to detect tool errors and all other manual or non-manual methods (for example it is possible to replay a generated code).

13.3.3.4.2. Evidence of proper functioning

Evidence of proper functioning can be translated by the use of a product with a certificate or by demonstrating that there is a return of experience.

13.3.3.4.3. Certified product

When a development language has a standard defining it, it is possible to implement a certification process that will lead to the establishment of a certificate defining the usage constraints and restrictions. It is worth noting that the certification of a compiler is a difficult activity and that all language standards are not associated with a standardized set of compliance tests.

Compilers are not the only tools that can be certified, a tool can also be certified in relation to a standard defining the realization process regarding a level of safety to be achieved.

The second case is becoming the most common, although it is quite difficult to explain how a standard applicable to the realization of a software application (IEC 61508, CENELEC EN 50128, etc.) that will be shipped in a real-time system is applicable to an executable application on a PC-type machine.

The C-code generator of the SCADE[1] environment (see Volume 3 [BOU 17a]) is a known and recognized example of tools with a certificate. The code generator named KCG in version 5 of the SCADE environment was the subject of a compliance certificate regarding the DO178 standard in B version [ARI 92]. In the context of version 6 of the SCADE environment, the C-code generator has been certified regarding DO 178:B [ARI 92], IEC 61508 [IEC 00, IEC 08] and CENELEC EN 50128 [CEN 01, CEN 11] standards.

When we have a certificate, it is necessary to identify the list of restrictions and usage constraints. The restrictions will be used to enrich the programming guide and the usage constraints will be used to verify and justify the safety file.

---

1 See http://www.esterel-technologies.com.

The existence of a certificate is certainly the easiest way, but what remains is to verify that the certificate is applicable to the use and that the exported constraints are assumed. The verification that the certificate is applicable is done through a *cross-acceptance* activity (Application guide of the CENELEC EN 50129 standard – Part 1 [CEN 07]), which will be carried out by the independent assessor.

"Cross-acceptance" is a phase that consists of verifying that the normative context, hypotheses and exported constraints of an evaluation report and/or of a certificate are compatible with the intended usage of the project.

13.3.3.4.4. Documented return of experience

If the tool is used in a very similar context (to be shown) over a long period of time (to be shown), it is possible to rely on the fact that the tool is "proven by use".

Techniques/measures	SIL2–SIL2	SIL3–SIL4
High confidence demonstrated by the use Optional when previous evidence is not available	R: 10,000 h of operation time and at least 1 year of experience with the equipment in operation	R: 1 million h of operation time, at least 2 years of experience with the different equipment including safety analyses, with the detailed documentation of minor modifications realized during the operation time

Table 13.10. *Table E.9 of the CENELEC EN 50129:2003 [CEN 03] standard*

The documented return of experience is to show the proper functioning of the tool through a formalization of previous experiences. This approach allows us to promote earlier uses and prepare for the future. This approach is consistent with the notion of high confidence demonstrated by the use introduced in Table E.9 of the CENELEC EN 50129:2003 standard (see Table 13.10).

The difficulty of the documented return of experience is related to the developments (too much and/or very fast) of the tools; it is quite difficult to ensure that a tool has the same behavior throughout these developments. From one version to the other, it is possible to rectify and add defects that will or will not have an impact on the behavior and usable services. Therefore, it is necessary to properly identify the services used or usable and have a process of acceptance of new versions (section 6.7.4.11 of the CENELEC EN 50128 standard).

For the documented return of experience, we should therefore put in place a continuous process. This process must recommend the use of already qualified tools; it must define an acceptance procedure of a new version and must recommend the upgrading of the documented return of experience at each end of project.

The documented return of experience can be a document in the form of a table as shown in Table 13.11.

Tools	Version	Fct	Project name	Nb of line	SSIL level	Date	Comment
Workshop B	3.04	Code generation	METEOR	100 000	SSIL4	Oct 98	First use

Table 13.11. *Example of a documented return of experience*

In the railway domain, concerning compilers, there is currently a certain return of experience that is documentable; these practices led to the evolution of tools only when necessary.

13.3.3.4.5. Validation

The validation of a tool is identified through the clause 6.7.4.5 of the CENELEC EN 50128:2011 standard. This clause recommends defining a validation strategy, which must focus on the list of usable services.

As for software validation, the validation of a tool is based on a set of tests, which must be complete regarding the specification (or the manual of use) and the list of usable services. The means used must be identified in order to replay the tests identically. The test scenarios and the results must be registered to allow the replay and auditing. It is necessary to formulate and formalize a judgment concerning the proper functioning of the tool's services. In the event of an anomaly, this version of the tool can be rejected or a new restricted functional perimeter can be defined.

13.3.3.4.6. Other

Documented return of experience and validation are the two approaches to privilege, but they are not always applicable. Indeed, faced with complex and innovative tools, such as automatic proof tools and abstract interpretation tools, it is difficult to have a return of experience and/or to implement a validation (especially when the algorithms are under *copyright*).

In this situation, it is then necessary to finely analyze the possible deficiencies and to imagine if it is possible to control them:

– through a realization process (combination of tools and activities);

– through a verification of the execution (for example a double compilation and a comparison of performances);

– through complementary activities such as manual verifications.

Clause 6.7.4.6 of the standard allows us to formalize a justification that should be documented and will be subject to the approval of the evaluator.

The first difficulty of this approach is linked to the reuse; the argument can depend very much on the project. The second difficulty is related to the fact that this approach is subject to discussion and is not guaranteed to converge with the evaluator toward an acceptance.

13.4. Adequacy to need

13.4.1. *Conception method*

The CENELEC EN 50128:2011 standard recommends that the conception method of the software be compatible with the characteristics of the application.

There are different types of paradigm to realize the conception and/or coding, such as the object-oriented approach (UML, OMT, etc.), the functional approach or the imperative approach. It is necessary to justify that the chosen approach is compatible with the application under development (software dashboard, etc.). The notion of compatibility is linked to the fact that a wrong approach risks making the realization of the model and its comprehension more complex, thus making the maintenance of the software more difficult.

The conception method and the programming language must allow for detecting errors as soon as possible, for example when compiling. That is why the C language is less suited than the Ada language. ADA [ADA 83, ADA 01, ISO 95] allows to detect, while compiling, typing errors and/or poor construction right from compiling and it guarantees typing control at execution.

Conception can rely on code generating tools allowing for the production of a partial code (signature of services, etc.) or a complete one. Code generation should be justified. Compilation must implement tools that are evaluated in accordance with the objectives (see T3 tools).

13.4.2. Method and language adequacy

If the conception method and the language used are not in accordance with the type of application being realized, it will be necessary to identify the weak points of the approach and propose measures to cover them up.

For example, the main difficulty of the C language resides in weak typing. Typing is summarized to handling types of bases such as the int (or similarly word, etc.). It is, therefore, necessary to compensate for the absence of a functional-related typing, for example x belongs to 1...10, by additional checks that will be introduced in the form of defensive programming (if $(x \geq 1$ and $x \leq 10)$ in entry of each function). This defensive programming complicates the code and therefore makes its maintenance more difficult.

13.4.3. Code generation

In the context of the implementation of the methods said to be "formal" or at least with model-oriented approaches, it is possible to automatically generate the code from a model. The CENELEC EN 50128:2011 standard requests that the adequacy of the code generation for the development of a software application of safety must be justified when the tool is selected.

If a model is used, it is possible to realize a number of verification activities on this model. The implementation of an automatic code generation activity allows for recuperating a code similar to the entry model. In the absence of a demonstration that the generated code is the exact image of the model (for example by using a certified code generator), it is necessary to carry out all the verifications as if the code had been written manually. If the code is shown as being the exact image of the model, it will be possible to justify that verification actions are not carried out on the generated code.

It is to be noted that code generation can be carried out to produce the generic application code and/or to produce the code related to the generic software application's configuration data.

13.5. Version management

For each tool, we must know the usable version(s) and the associated usage constraints (see Figure 13.5).

13.5.1. *Identification of versions*

It is necessary to identify each version that is qualified. This identification must be as precise as possible. We should be careful to properly identify the set of "patches" that could be applied to obtain the qualified version.

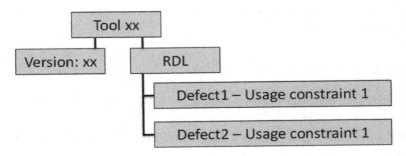

Figure 13.5. *Tool version management*

13.5.2. *Analysis of defects*

For each version, there exists a list of residual defects, i.e. the residual defect list (RDL). It is therefore necessary to carry out this RDL analysis in order to identify the use constraints of the tool. The use constraints may imply functions to not use, implementation precautions, limits (for example, a maximum number of files that the tool can process in one session).

13.5.3. *Change of version*

There are different reasons to change the version of a tool:

– change in version;

– BUG correction;

– patch application;

– non-maintained version (see obsolete).

It is necessary to define a clear policy to manage the evolution of a tool. Some examples of policies are as follows:

– without warning and waiting for the reaction of users;

– qualification of the new version;

– demonstration of the non-impact:

– comparison of the generated executable bit-to-bit;

– replay of the activities carried out on the previous version;

– back-to-back verification.

The management process of the versions should identify the process of acceptance of a new version. This process is based on:

– the identification of the version;

– the identification of the evolutions: functional evolutions, list of options, etc.

– the demonstration that the evolutions do not affect the compatibility of the tool with the process implemented on the project(s);

– the analysis of the new RDL (closure of default and thus removal of use-associated constraints, new defects and addition of new use constraints).

Concerning the third point, we may need to implement the replay test used in the initial qualification.

13.6. Qualification process

13.6.1. *Tool qualification report*

The qualification process such as the CENELEC EN 50128:2011 standard introduced must give rise to a qualification file associated with each tool. This qualification file is to be realized, not at the project level but that of the company, in order to use it on several projects and thus to strengthen confidence in the tools at the discretion of their implementation.

13.6.2. *At the end*

Concerning the rail industry, the 2011 version of the CENELEC EN 50128 standard is not yet mandatory but it is preferable to implement it because unlike the 2001 version, it sets a formal framework for the qualification of tools. Indeed, it sets objective and identifies means to implement them.

It should be noted that concerning the qualification of tools, almost all the industries in the rail area have implemented a process of qualification of tools.

13.6.3. *Qualification of non-commercial tools*

The process described in section 13.3.3 is easily applicable to tools of commerce, but it is in a more difficult manner applicable to tools developed in a local, or even for a specific project. In general, for non-commercial tools, it is necessary to put in place a realization process that is consistent with the business standards.

Business standards (CENELEC 50128:2011, DO 178, IEC 61508, ISO 26262) being oriented toward onboard applications, it is not always easy to implement them completely during the development of a tool. This is why the DO 330 [RTA 11b] approach might be interesting, although not directly applicable in the rail industry.

13.7. Conclusion

One of the main advances of business trades (CENELEC 50128:2011, DO 178, IEC 61508, ISO 26262) concerns the class introduction for the tools implied in the realization process of a software application and the definition of qualification objectives for each class.

In this chapter, we presented requirements and gave elements in order to achieve the qualification file of each tool.

As we have already indicated, the IEC 62279:2014 [IEC 14] standard introduces Table 10.3 by completing the requests of the CENELEC 50128:2011. In preparation for the new CENELEC 50126 [CEN 12] standard, section 7.9 increases the number of requirements from 12 to 17. The new requirements do not change the process that has been discussed in this chapter; they concern the need to select the appropriate tools, to have tools that cooperate and are compatible with the product or the process, that the tools are available, etc.

Data Configured Software Application

14.1. Introduction

In recent years, the development of software-based systems underwent changes induced by the need to develop product lines. Indeed, a product is not only destined for a use (see the case of subway lines) but must be able to be used in different settings. For example, the VAL (Automatic Light Vehicle)[1] of the company Siemens Transportation System was put into service in Lille, Toulouse, Charles de Gaulle Airport, etc., and each time it offers shared services, specific services and a route topology associated with each site. This problem is common to the different areas and associated standards [BAU 11].

When a system is dependent on a set of data to define and implement its behavior, we say that it is a parameterized system. Parameters can be of different types: data describing the context of the system (topology, speed curve, breakpoints, etc.), service data settings (maximum number of items, weight, etc.) and activation/inhibition of services data.

Within the framework of parameterized systems, the safety of the complex, critical and reliable system is not only based on the validation of

---

1 The VAL is a light subway train present in many places in France. The first VAL was inaugurated at Lille in 1983. It serves today the cities of Taipei and Toulouse, Rennes and Turin (since January 2006). Concerning the deployment of the VAL, there is at least 119 km of lines that are deployed in the world with 830 cars in operation or construction. The VAL CDG combines the technology of the VAL and of the complementary digital equipment based on the B method [ABR 96].

the software application but also on the validation of the data handled by the software application.

The purpose of this chapter is to present the problems of management (definition, verification and validation) of data handled by a critical system. Note that the control of parameterized software applications is explicitly introduced in the railway standards dedicated to software or the CENELEC EN 50128 [CEN 01, CEN 11] and IEC 62279 [IEC 14].

14.2. Problem

The global positioning system (GPS) is a tool used in everyday life and a system where data are omnipresent. For the GPS, we do not imagine direct impacts on safety, although there may be some surprising situations (absence of routes, non-optimal route or contrary to signage, etc., as shown in Figure 14.1) but the driver remains responsible of his decisions, it is only a driving aid. New uses of the GPS, such as the positioning of the trains, might have an impact on the recommendations related to safety such as the measurement of position, accuracy, etc.

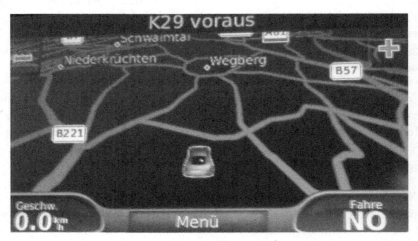

Figure 14.1. *Example of data-related problems*

As we shall see below, railways are a major example where data are ubiquitous in the realization of the system, but these are not the only systems. The nuclear, automobile and space domains are domains where data control can have an impact on safety.

For example, in the nuclear field, the notion of parameterization data is essential. Thus, separation and incineration in reactor (SPIN) systems and monitoring units (MU) of N4[2] reactors manage a large amount of data (more than 10,000). Some of them are updated during the reactor's operation to take into account the wear of the fuel in particular. At least two incidents in relation to the data are identified on the ASN website (Nuclear Safety Authority, www.asn.fr). Following the incidents of February 14, 2000 and April 4, 2000, analysis showed that it was parameterization errors that have led to an underestimation of the power generated by the fuel in a given situation, which led to automatic reactor shutdowns. Note that these are the parameters of the SPIN and the MU. These errors were due to the poor quality of the documentation used for the systems' programming.

In the nuclear field, section 5.2 of the IEC 60880 standard [IEC 06] introduced the concept of configuration data as the data necessary for the adaptation of software applications to input/output and services required by the installation. The parameterization data are classified into two families:

– data that are not intended to be changed online by operators and are subject to the same requirements as the rest of the software;

– the parameters; in other words, data that can be modified by the operators during the installation's operation (e.g. alarm thresholds, control points, calibration of instrumentation data) and have specific requirements.

In the field of aerospace, the preparation of an Ariane 5 flight [BOU 09b, Chapter 7] requires the production of data related to a trajectory. These data should reflect the characteristics of the launcher, the identified trajectory and meteorological conditions. The data are of three types: mission data (mass, orbit parameters, etc.), family data (cap type, etc.), configuration data and data dependent on the launcher (sensor calibration, etc.). Before you can process the data, it is necessary to carry out studies and simulations. The data (tabulated) are produced as an Ada package [ANS 83, ISO 95, BAR 14] exploitable by the flight program.

---

2 The N4 is a 1,450 MWe water pressure reactor operated by EDF.

14.3. System parameterized by data

14.3.1. *Presentation of the problem*

Control/command systems currently being developed are becoming bigger; they introduce the concept of communication and they are data consumers.

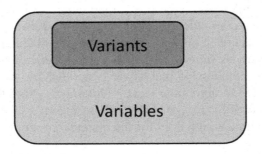

Figure 14.2. *Variables and variants*

Within software applications, it is possible to handle two types of data, constant and variable (global, local, function parameters, function returns, etc.). The variables acquired from the environment are called "variants" (see Figure 14.2) and they allow characterization of the state of the software application's environment at time T (see definition 14.1).

DEFINITION 14.1.– (VARIANT). *A variant is a software's variable that represents data of the environment. This variable is acquired by the software application, which can change value at each cycle.*

The number of objects of a family is a constant for a software version but it might be necessary to make it evolve over time following a system extension. To do this, it is necessary to be able to change a constant and produce a new version of the software application without having to redo all verifications (proofreading, testing, etc.). This constant is then called a parameter of the software application and seen as static (constant) during the execution.

The parameters of software application are static date constants (see Figure 14.3), which can be of two types:

– fixed data, called invariant, characterizing the environment (topology, trajectory, etc.), the system (number of items, limit, etc.) and the characteristics (weight, length, speed, etc.);

– data evolving with the system's state (wear, extension, etc.).

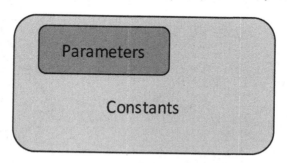

Figure 14.3. *Constant sand parameters*

DEFINITION 14.2.– (PARAMETER). *A parameter is a constant for a given instance of a software application. These data can be modified to produce another version of the application or can be changed before execution to reflect the system's status.*

A configurable software application is divided into two parts, generic application and parameterization. The instance of the generic application for a given use is called *specific application.*

DEFINITION 14.3.– (SPECIFIC APPLICATION). *One specific application is a generic application to which a parameterization has been associated. This specific application is usable only for a single installation.*

Note that the notion of specific application covers the software and hardware aspects. The hardware is a fixed characteristic (an input in the realization of the software, see Figure 14.4, and software is validated for a platform). It is then possible to define the generic application (see definition 14.4).

DEFINITION 14.4.– (GENERIC APPLICATION). *A generic application consists of an execution platform (called generic product), a software application and a parameterization process. This software application is defined in accordance with a parameter data set that will be instantiated based on the final use (depending on the site, the services to be enabled, the technical characteristics, etc.).*

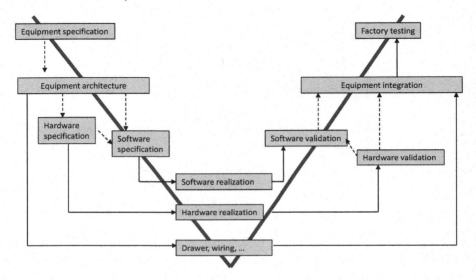

Figure 14.4. *Complete development cycle*

Definition 14.4 identifies the specific application as composed of three parts, and among the latter the parameterization process is a delicate point subject of this chapter. The concept of generic application covers the concept of non-parameterized software; as there is no instantiation, there is no specific application.

As shown in Figure 14.5, the generic application is then the composition of generic software and an execution platform. The execution platform is called a generic product and covers hardware and software aspects (operating system, basic software, middleware layer for managing communications, etc.).

DEFINITION 14.5.– (GENERIC PRODUCT). *A generic product is composed of a set of hardware elements and a set of software. It aims to allow the execution of a software application. A generic product can be used for the realization of different systems.*

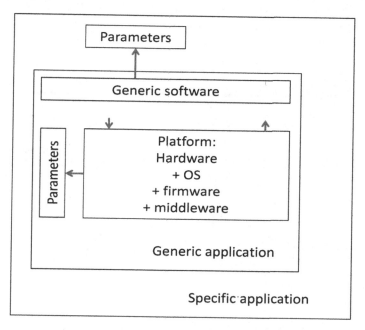

Figure 14.5. *Configured system*

As indicated in Definition 14.5, a generic product is intended to run different types of software applications, the generic side allows flexibility, the notion of product is related to the fact that this set can be certified independently of the field of use and is, for example, the case of programmable controllers.

Invariant data are known to the system's generation and define a system's configuration. It is thus possible to define a system generically and to implant it through a parameterization on another site.

For example, from the description of a subway line, it is possible to derive a set of data that will be common to all of the system's equipment. These data depend on the topology of the line, characteristics of the trains and technological choices (response time, CPU processing time, etc.). In the railway field, these are called "topological invariants" [GEO 90].

As shown in Figure 14.5, we can have different levels of configuration. In Figure 14.6, some parameters are related to the generic product (memory size, IP address, processing time, etc.) and some parameters are related to the generic application.

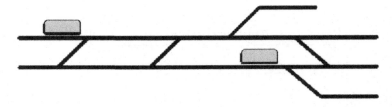

Figure 14.6. *Example of topology*

A railway line (see the fictitious example introduced in Figure 14.6) is made up of several tracks. Trains use tracks to move from one point to another. A track is made up of several track circuits (TCs).

A TC is a physically defined portion of track that detects the presence of trains by "shunting"[3].

A basic TC (a branch) has the following characteristics:

– beginning and end;

– State (shunted, non-shunted);

– previous TC, next TC.

Figure 14.7. *Static and dynamic definitions of a point machine*

---

3 The track circuit has a power supply. When two wheels of the same axle of a train are in the zone delimited by the track circuit, a short circuit occurs, and the train is said to be shunting the track circuit. The main function of the track circuit is to detect shunting.

A single abscissa reference point is defined by deconstructing the line. Each position (track object or train) is characterized by a pair (track number, abscissa). Passages from one track to another are carried out using a point machine. A point machine (see Figure 14.7) is a three-branch TC, made up of a fixed component and a mobile component (the point). A point has three logical States uncontrolled (operational fault detected), in a straight position, or in a divergent position.

A switch can therefore be seen as a TC, and presents the following characteristics:

– TC characteristics:

  - Point abscissa, divergent abscissa, direct abscissa;

  - TC following point, TC following direct, TC following divergent;

  - State: shunted, non-shunted.

– Switch characteristics:

  - Type: right, left;

  - State: direct, divergent, uncontrolled.

Due to this complexity of data, we chose the railway domain as a support of our study, but all the work presented in the context of this chapter shall be applied to other areas where data are important because of their size (e.g. GPS data) and due to their use (e.g. precise localization).

14.3.2. Characterization of data

A specific application (see definition 14.3) is then dedicated for a use. This application uses data that can be of different natures:

– data for the activation/inhibition of services;

– fixed data that do not change over time; they describe the system's characteristics (topology, speed curve, breakpoints, etc.);

– the data that change over time; the time of evolution is the largest cycle or duration.

Data evolving regularly (in the railway field, these data are called "variant") can be:

– inputs that the system acquires regularly;

– data that the system calculates as global or local variables and system outputs.

DEFINITION 14.6.– (CONFIGURATION DATA). *Configuration data are data that do not change during the execution of the software application.*

As indicated in Definition 14.6, the configuration data (in the railway field we call it invariant) is a first type of data. The configuration data include data regrouping usually two families that define the technical characteristics (speed, weight, size, number, etc.) and data defining the context of use (topology, velocity curves, stopping points, etc.).

The configuration data characterizes the implementation of a so-called generic software application for a specific case. Note that there are two types of parameterized data (see Figure 14.8): calibration data that in view of their very slow evolution are considered invariant and configuration data that are really invariant.

DEFINITION 14.7.– (CALIBRATION DATA). *Calibration data are data that evolve according to a "large" time unit.*

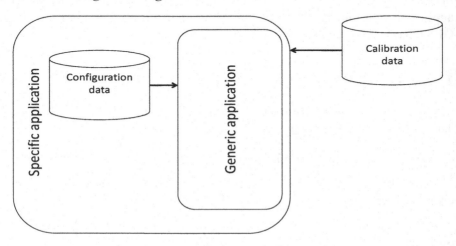

Figure 14.8. *Configuration versus calibration data*

As indicated in Definition 14.7, the calibration data are related to the fact that the system characteristics change over time (reduction of fissile material in the case of a nuclear power plant, changing engine characteristics due to wear, etc.). Railway systems do not use calibration data.

14.3.3. *Inhibition of service*

The configuration data may be associated with the system's actual data, but in some cases they are associated with services such as inhibition/activation data. These (see Figure 14.9) allow or prevent the execution of services.

The use of inhibition/activation data is then associated with the notion of dead code (not executable in actual execution). It is then necessary to have a complete validation of the application with and without the functions controlled by the data to ensure that a failure of execution (memory anomaly processor anomaly, mismanagement of a pointer, etc.) cannot place the software application in a non-controlled situation.

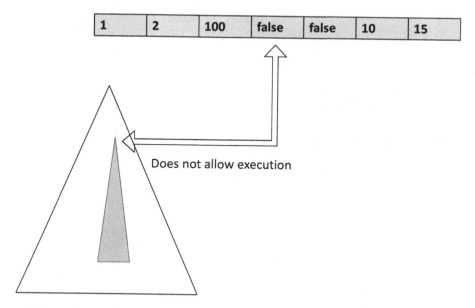

Figure 14.9. *Data controlling the activation of a code's portion*

These types of data make it possible to establish a capitalization activity and thus to set up a service reutilization process that is already controlled, but it is not compatible with realizing *a priori* of functions unnecessary for future use. As much as this approach can reduce the cost of future projects through reuse of existing projects, it may increase in an uncontrolled manner the development cost of functions not used *a priori* in the project.

The inhibition/activation data are useful for defining a product line. Figure 14.10 shows an application execution process based on the concept of product lines. The generic product is not a separate application; it is necessary to implement a step of specialization that defines the common perimeter between the core and the generic application to realize; from here, it is possible to build the generic application on a common base.

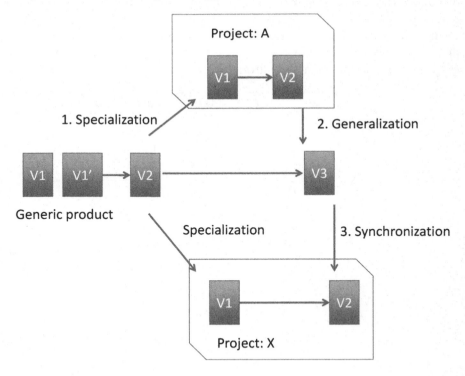

Figure 14.10. *Product lines*

This process is associated with two activities:

– The first activity, that we can name the generalization, allows bringing the behavior of the generic application that has been validated in the core; we can then use them in a future software development.

– The second activity is called synchronization and is linked to the fact of upgrading a generic application with respect to the common trunk. Indeed, the common trunk may have evolved (defect correction, generalization, etc.).

We will not describe further the concept of product lines, even if it remains a challenge to control the cost of implementing software applications. Domain standards such as DO 178, CENELEC EN 50128 [CEN 01, CEN 11], ISO 26262, etc., do not identify this problem.

14.3.4. *Synthesis*

This section allows implementing a vocabulary adapted to parametric software applications. Within the railway sector, the concepts of generic product and generic and specific application allow reuse, but they are especially crucial to partition safety studies.

In terms of domain standards, only the railway field introduced the concepts of generic and specific application. The CENELEC 50126 [CEN 00][4] standard – which describes the control of the safety process – applies from the complete system to the generic one and the CENELEC 50129 standard [CEN 03] – which focuses on the formalization of the safety demonstration – introduces the concept of *safety cases* and the possibility of realizing safety cases for the generic product, the generic and/or specific application.

Finally, at the level of business standards, only the railway field allows the realization of systems based on generic products, generic and/or specific applications and uses only configuration-type parameterization data.

---

4 See Chapter 3, for an introduction to the CENELEC standards and particularly to the CENELEC 50129 standard and the notion of safety file.

14.4. From the system to the software

14.4.1. *Requirement*

Parameterized software applications require specific work to identify and develop data that are manipulated. This activity is now identified as an activity to be realized in the implementation phase of the software application, but there is the risk of building a system that will not work.

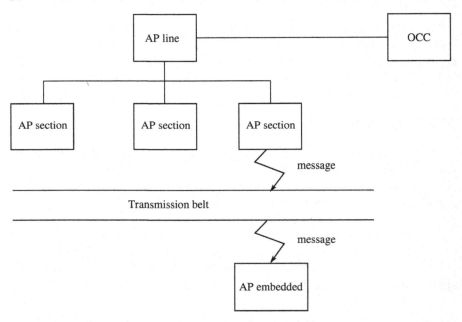

Figure 14.11. *System vision*

Indeed, an automatic subway system (see, for example[5], Figure 14.11) consists of equipment (OCC, AP-Line, AP-Section, AP-Embedded and communication) that may have multiple software applications that are parameterized or not (see Figure 14.12).

---

5 The presented example is related to the SAET-METEOR [MAT 98] deployed on line 14 of the Paris subway; for more information, refer to [BOU 11b, Chapter 2].

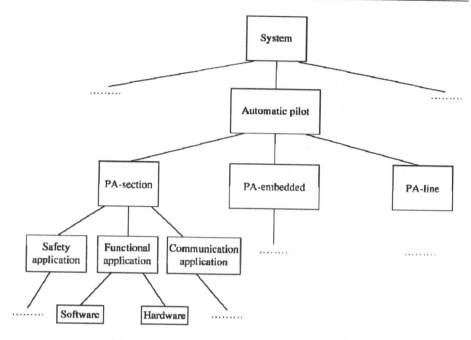

Figure 14.12. *From the system to the software*

In such an approach, the main difficulty is in the consistency of data between devices. The data must (note that this list that is not exhaustive but can give an idea of the problem):

– describe the same system: common source in input of the production data, the same version of the data, the same interpretation of the characteristics of the data, etc.;

– be consistent: compatible accuracy, same reference units (km, etc.), similar repository for tracking (where is the point of reference?, etc.), compatibility of references (passing a marker in KP track markings, etc.; see Figure 14.13), identical boundaries (the maximum train speed should be the same for all equipments, etc.);

– be correct: a common validation activity must show that the data are correct and that the behavior of the system complies with what is required for all configurations.

Figure 14.13 shows a sample topology and it is possible to have different standards for the tracking of objects. Initially, the tracking of objects is achieved through a measure in relation to kilometric points (denoted KP, see case (A) in Figure 14.13), but in terms of equipment, we tend to work on benchmarks that are more accurate such as the local segment (case (B) in Figure 14.14) or the track identification.

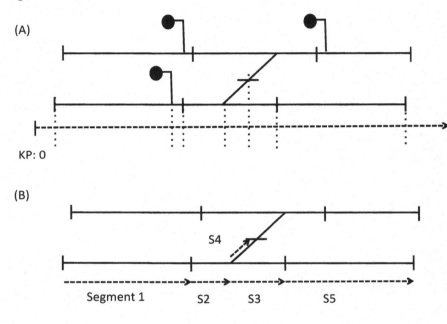

Figure 14.13. *Object positioning: A) from a KP; B) from a segment*

14.4.2. *What the CENELEC standard does not say*

The concept of information is essential to the railway system, but the CENELEC 50126 [CEN 00] standard that describes the safety control process throughout the system's lifecycle does not directly mention this concept and the CENELEC 50129 [CEN 03] standard that aims to formalize the safety demonstration introduces well the concept of generic product and generic application but without indicating how and in what form the parameterization must be managed.

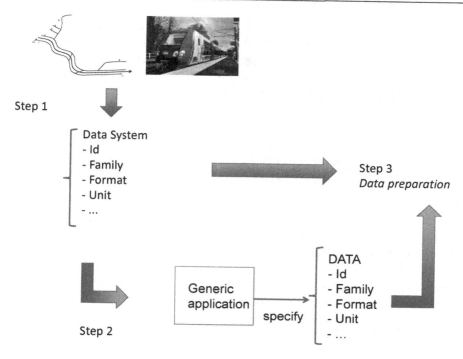

Figure 14.14. *A three-stage process*

As shown in Figure 14.13, the data preparation process to be implemented consists of three stages:

– Stage 1: Identification of the system/subsystem/equipment data. This identification allows defining the data and their characteristics;

– Stage 2: Identification of data consumed by the generic software. Based on data from the system and the needs of the software, during the software's design, we must identify the data that are actually consumed and their characteristics;

– Stage 3: Definition of the data production process. based on the system data and the data necessary to parameterize the generic application, a data preparation process must be defined. It will show that the data from the data preparation processes respect the expected properties. These data production processes shall demonstrate that the data meet its safety objectives [BOU 99, BOU 00].

The data preparation process was identified in the previous version of the CENELEC EN 50128:2001 [CEN 01] standard, but it was impractical. In the 2011 version of the standard, section 8 identifies the principles that characterize the data and the requirements to make a data preparation process that respects the CENELEC EN 50128:2011 [CEN 11] standard (or the IEC 62279 [IEC14] standard) and the software safety integrity level (SSIL) objective. Regarding other business standards, the automotive ISO 26262 standard also introduces the need to manage the parameterization data but it does not propose specific processes.

14.5. Data preparation process

As we have said many times, the different domain standards show the need to have parameterized software applications. The railway and automotive sectors are the two domains where the standards introduce the need to develop a data production process, but the railway standards (CENELEC 50128 and IEC 62279) explicitly introduce this process (activities, documents, organization). We chose to present this process as part of this chapter.

Within the framework of this section, we present the data preparation process as provided by the CENELEC EN 50128:2011 standard and we will specifically explain the expectations related to section 8 of this standard.

14.5.1. *Context*

14.5.1.1. *Software quality assurance*

The software quality assurance is to be implemented both for the realization of generic software application and the parameterization. It is therefore necessary to have quality assurance in accordance with ISO 9001:2015 [ISO 15], a control of competencies, an organization, a configuration management, verification/validation, to qualify the tools and realize an evaluation.

We must therefore have a set of plans (software quality assurance plan (SQAP), software configuration management plan (SCMP), software verification and validation plan (SVVP), etc.) to describe the organization, processes and resources used to realize the data preparation process. These plans may be specific or not, data preparation can be a part of a project or a full project.

The software assurance was presented as part of Chapter 5 and is applicable to generic software, to the realization of data preparation process, or to application of the data preparation process for one instantiation.

14.5.1.2. Management of safety assurance

The CENELEC EN 50128:2011 standard does not identify any safety assurance but it requires the implementation of the CENELEC 50126 [CEN 00] standard. The CENELEC 50126 standard defines a management cycle of the RAMS that goes from the acquisition of the need to the system's withdrawal. What is important to us is that the CENELEC 50126 standard requires that the safety team identify safety functional requirements and the safety integrity requirements, and to follow all the requirements throughout the cycle.

The CENELEC 50129 [CEN 03] standard, regarding the safety record and that is normally applicable to the signaling subsystem (in the next version of the CENELEC 50126 standard, this section will be applicable to all parts of the system), introduced various safety record levels:

– the generic product's safety record;

– the generic application's safety case;

– the specific application's safety case.

This structure is consistent with Figure 14.4 and definitions 14.4–14.6, which were introduced earlier.

The safety team must define its safety assurance plan (SAP), a safety demonstration strategy that takes into account this decomposition. A set of activities will be set up to demonstrate that:

– the management of safety requirements is performed in each level;

– the generic product is safe and that it clearly identifies the exported constraints linked to its use;

– the generic application assumes the exported constraints of the generic product that it is safe and clearly identifies the exported constraints linked to its use;

– the specific application assumes the exported constraints of the generic product that it is safe and clearly identifies the exported constraints linked to its use;

– the specific application is consistent with the final installation.

14.5.2. *Presentation of section 8 of the CENELEC EN 50128:2011 standard*

14.5.2.1. *Lifecycle*

In general, the standards recommend the V cycle as a cycle to implement for the realization of a software application. For section 8 of the CENELEC EN 50128:2011 standard, the cycle to implement is different. Indeed, the production process of the parameterization data was seen as a whole. Section 8.2 identifies inputs, section 8.3 identifies the outputs and section 8.4 describes the cycle (see Figure 14.13) and activities to realize in this cycle.

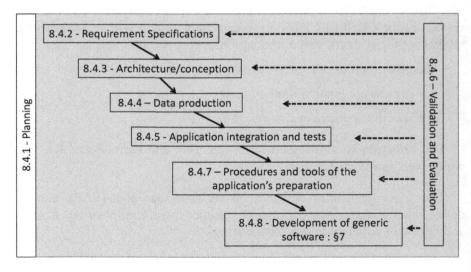

Figure 14.15. *Data preparation cycle*

The data preparation cycle is a cycle that resembles the cascade cycle and it is composed of eight phases. Among these eight phases, there are three particular phases:

– the planning phase (8.4.1) that aims to define the data preparation strategy, operations, documentation to produce and the means;

– the validation and evaluation phase (8.4.6), which is not really only one phase. Indeed, the only associated article indicates that we must monitor the performance of each phase of the development cycle. As the implementation of ISO 9001 is required, this phase is covered by the verification activities that must be implemented. This is why, in Figure 14.15, it appears on the right as a control activity of the end of each phase;

– the generic application's development phase (8.4.8), which refers to section 7 of the CENELEC EN 50128 standard and introduces the parameterization-related recommendations.

14.5.2.2. *Problem of circularity*

Within the framework of section 8.2 regarding the input documents, it is stated that it is necessary to have, at the input of the data production process, the specification of requirements, architecture, application conditions and the generic software's user manual, which suggests that the generic software is already realized and the data preparation process remains to be defined.

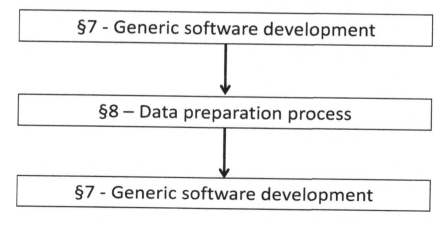

Figure 14.16. *Circularity between generic software and data preparation*

Section 8.8 of the standard concerns the development of the generic software. It refers directly to section 7 after having identified additional recommendations related to the parameterization data. As shown in Figure 14.16, there seems to be circularity in the process.

In fact, the circularity is induced by the fact that there are several possibilities for developing software and the parameterization data as shown in Figure 14.17. In case 1, we first realize the generic application and on this basis we can then develop the data. On the other hand, case 2 is designed to perform data preparation and then to develop the generic application.

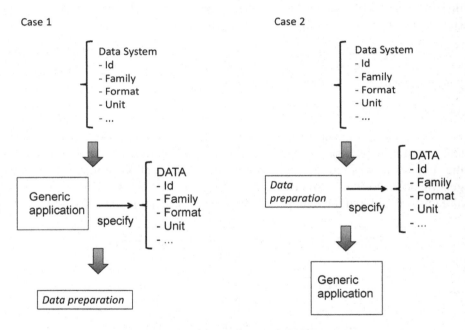

Figure 14.17. *Various realization processes*

From another point of view, in the railway sector, there are currently two approaches concerning the format of the parameterization data:

– The first approach, which corresponds to case 1 in Figure 14.18, called "tabular data": based on the algorithms identified in the generic software, we construct specific data tables dedicated to the algorithms. This approach optimizes execution time and reduces the complexity of algorithms, but it is difficult to find the system data in the tables and the data time becomes very large. This type of approach has been developed on the SACEM [GEO 90] MAGGALY [May 93], the SAET-METEOR [BOU 00, BOU 06, DEL 99], the VAL of CdG, etc.

– The second approach, which corresponds to case 2 in Figure 14.18, is called "domain-specific data": from the input documents, we produce parameterization data files that are centered on the domain and find objects of the system. A high-level language (state machine, Petri nets, etc.) is used to describe each object, these various states and links with other objects. The generic software is then an execution machine of objects that must respect the semantics of the high-level language that was used. This type of approach has been implemented on PAING [BOU 11b, Chapters 4 and 6] and the PMI [GAL 08]. In this case, at the end of application of Chapter 8 we need to develop the algorithms related to the domain-specific data.

The choice of one of the two strategies determines the type of generic applications to realize and the overall realization process of the final software application.

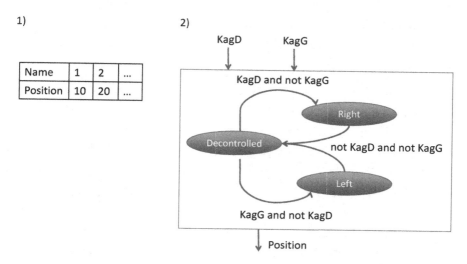

Figure 14.18. *Example of data*

In case 1 in Figure 14.18, the reality is somewhat more complex. In general, the generic data and software are developed in parallel. The parallelism is induced by the fact that during the realization of the software, it may be necessary to introduce:

– specific data to control algorithms;

– data with specific characteristics that allow the optimization of the software's performance and/or the reduction of the algorithms' complexity. In the context of complex algorithms with multiple element searches, it may be preferable to simplify the algorithms and to generate specific data tabulated in this algorithm; the complexity is then transferred from the algorithm executed by the generic software to the data generation algorithm.

Finally, we see that section 8.2 of the CENELEC EN 50128:2011 standard must be completed with all the systems' documents allowing the identification of data. The systems' documents must describe the data from the system's point of view.

14.6. Data preparation process

14.6.1. *Data preparation process control*

14.6.1.1. *Planification*

Within the framework of this section, we will deal with stage 8.4.1 called planification. It is recommended to realize a preparation plan for the application called APP.

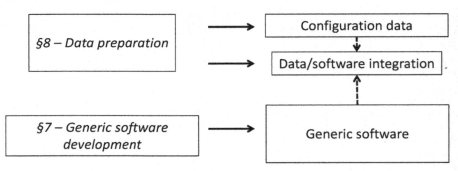

Figure 14.19. *Link between the two processes of realization*

Figure 14.19 shows that the preparation of the data must manage two types of activities: the production of parameterization data and integration of data with the generic software. This is why the APP is to be realized either for each specific application or for a specific application class. If it is produced for a specific application class, we will finally validate a configuration family.

As for the SQAP, the APP must:

– choose between business data and tabular data;

– describe the application development process (see sections 14.6.1.2 and 14.6.1.3);

– describe the human resources, the organization and independences;

– for each phase of the process, identify activities to be realized, the input and output documents and human resources to implement;

– for each phase of the process, identify verifications to be realized;

– identify the document structure;

– identify the tools that are implemented;

– describe the principles of configuration management.

The software's assurance, as defined in clause 6 of the CENELEC EN 50128:2011 standard, identifies a tree that can be common or not with data preparation. The APP can thus be composed of a single document or rely on other documents (SQAP, SDP, SCMP, SVVP, etc.).

Measure	SSIL0	SSIL1 SSIL2	SSIL3 SSIL4
1. Methods of specification in tables	R	R	R
2. Language specific to the application	R	R	R
3. Simulation	R	HR	HR
4. Functional testing	M	M	M
5. Checklists	R	HR	M
6. Fagan inspection	–	R	R
7. Formal design reviews	R	HR	HR
8. Formal proof of data correctness	–	–	HR
9. Structured Project review	R	R	HR

Table 14.1. *Table A.11 of the CENELEC 50128:2011 standard*

The CENELEC 50128:2011 standard identifies a number of techniques to implement for data preparation through Table A.11. Table A.11 shows two techniques:

– languages (1 and 2);

– the means of verification (3–9)[6].

One of the problems of preparing data concerns the means of expression to specify the data (clause 8.4.1.11, Table A.11 items 1 and 2). Indeed, the data can take different forms such as tabular data or domain specific data (Graphcet Petri network, etc.).

The APP should identify formalism to describe the data and the data production process, so that it is feasible and understandable, to limit the introduction of defects and to be repeatable and maintainable.

14.6.1.2. *Integration between data and the generic software*

The link between the data and the generic software is an important point that must be controlled. The generic software is a consumer of data; it can export constraints (see clause 8.4.16 of the standard) that data must comply to (always finish a table with the value −1, express distances in centimeters, etc.) and these constraints can be directly related to safety software.

There are different levels of integration between the parameterization data and the generic software as shown in Figure 14.20. Case 1 shows an example of software where the parameterization data are scattered or completely embedded in the software. In case 2, the parameterization data are a whole set but it remains integrated with the application. In case 3, the parameterization data are outside the software.

Figure 14.20. *Software integration level*

---

6 See Chapter 5 for a description of verification techniques.

The identification of the parameterization data, the principle of separation between the data and the generic software and interfaces, must be identified when specifying the generic software (clauses 8.4.8.2 and 8.4.8.3 of the standard).

Case 3 is interesting (see clause 8.4.8.4 of the standard) because it simplifies maintenance operations – a modification of data may not result in recompilation – but it introduces problems of integrity control and validity of data. Indeed, the executable protections do not cover the software, it is necessary to establish specific protections for the parameterization data and control mechanisms by the executable of the data's validity. The problem is "how does the software know that an integrated configuration (set of consistent data) is a correct configuration for it?".

14.6.1.3. Data production process

The data production process aims to transform (see Figure 14.21) system level data to data handled by the software. This transformation can be realized manually or tooled.

Figure 14.21. *Data transformation*

If the amount of data is small, it is possible to manually generate the parameterization data files. If the number is too large, it is preferable in order to control efforts and to ensure repeatability to tool the process.

The specification of the generic software must identify the level of SSIL, the software requirements and data. Thus, it is possible to identify the safety level of the parameterization data.

We must now define the data production process; the main difficulty is related to the correction of the transformation and it is possible to use three approaches [BOU 07] for the production of data (see Figure 14.22).

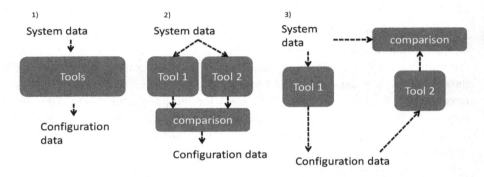

Figure 14.22. *Data transformation*

The first case consists of developing only one tool to produce the data. The second case consists of three tools; two diverse tools – but with the same specification – perform the same transformation and a comparator to verify that the result is identical (or similar in the case of partial comparison). The latter case consists of realizing a tool that does the processing and a tool that reverses the transformation and is completed with a comparator that verifies that the result is similar (in general, the transformations do not preserve all the information and so are unable to verify the equality).

The third case in Figure 14.22 ensures greater diversity (two different specifications) between the two tools than the second case (same specification).

We thus have at least four possible approaches, but they must be combined with the ability to manually verify data as in Table 14.2.

To these three approaches, it is possible to add one that focuses on verification through proof. Figure 14.23 shows two paths, the first is related to the generation of data and the second to the proof of data. The first chain is generally difficult to qualify (database usage, etc.); we link safety to the proof of data.

Production	Data verification	Characteristics	Comments
Manual	Manual (Re-read, etc.)	Limited data	The amount of data is manageable and eliminates the need of tools
Manual	Tests	Limited data	It is possible to show that the data are correct through comprehensive software testing. This approach is not feasible in the case of large amounts of data.
Tooled – case 1	Manual (Re-read, etc.)	Limited data	The limited amount of data allows for manual verification
Tooled – case 1		SSIL2 or SSIL3–4 data	A unique tool developed at data's SSIL level
Tooled – case 2		SSIL2 or SSIL3–4 data	We have a double chain that enables the use of tools for an SSIL (function diversification) inferior to the SSIL for the expected data
Tooled – case 3		SSIL2 or SSIL3–4 data	We have a double highly diversified chain that allows the use of tools of a SSIL inferior to the SSIL of the expected data
–	Tooled	SSIL2 or SSIL3–4 data	Data safety can be based on the implementation of a data verification tool (e.g. via proof)

Table 14.2. *Combinations for the realization of a data production process*

From the safety point of view, the efficiency of the proof of data is based on the properties to be proved. The chain of proof is doubled to ensure the outcome and to facilitate the qualification. This approach makes it possible to put the qualification effort on the chain of proof that will be T3 and to decrease the effort on the generation tool that will be T2 or T1.

The APP shall describe the data production process to implement depending on the SSIL level and identify all the tools to implement. For each tool, it is to either be realized or reused. In all cases (clause 8.4.1.10 of the standard), safety objectives (SIL, ASIL SSIL, DAL, etc.) and a qualification class (T1, T2 and T3) must be associated with the tool and a qualification of tools must be implemented in accordance with Chapter 13.

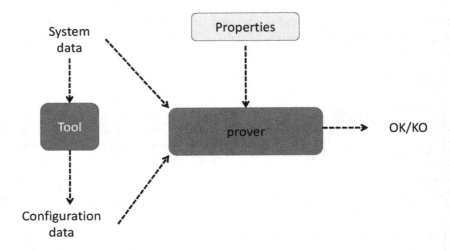

Figure 14.23. *Proof on data*

14.6.1.4. *Inputs of the data preparation process*

As we have explained in previous sections, section 8.2 of the CENELEC EN 50128:2011 standard does not identify all the input documents of the data production process. First, we must have as input the system documents listed below.

These documents must take into account the system's data, such as:

– specification of the system requirements;

– system architecture description;

– specification of the system's safety requirements.

In addition following the case in Figure 14.22 that is taken into account, we must at least have a SQAP that describes the process of realizing the specific application, the stages (software development, development of the data preparation process, data production, etc.) and the scheduling of these steps.

14.6.1.5. *Safety study of the data process*

The data production process is based on tools (see Figure 14.21), which are either reused or developed. The data are handled by generic software that will be developed for safety purposes (DAL, SSIL, etc.); it is thus necessary for the data to be as safe as the software that consumes it.

Clause 8.4.1.8 recommends performing a safety analysis on the proposed data preparation process to confirm that we can achieve the level of safety expected for the data. This safety analysis will confirm the expected levels of qualification, tools and safety level objectives (DAL, SSIL, etc.) allocated to them.

14.6.1.6. *Synthesis*

Finally (see Figure 14.24), before producing the APP, there must be a SQAP that describes the overall strategy to realize the specific application (development of a generic application, data production, instantiation of a configuration, creation of a specific application) and the scheduling of these activities. This SQAP must also identify the type of data (tabulated or profession) and the principles of data integration with the generic software.

From the SQAP, it is possible to produce the APP that must also define the organization, processes and resources; identify the data preparation process (see Table 14.2), identify the tools to be reused and develop and identify the level of qualification of tools and their SSIL objectives (safety study).

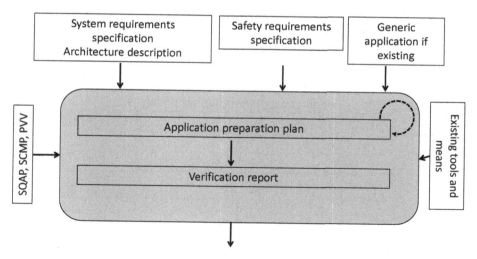

Figure 14.24. *The PPA and its verification*

As demanded by the ISO 9001:2015 standard, each product should be verified, the CENELEC EN 50128:2011 standard identifies a data verification report (DVR). The APP must be verified (compliance to the CENELEC EN 50128:2011 standard, coherence and implementation of each specific application). The results of this verification must be recorded in the DVR.

14.6.2. *Verification*

In Chapter 11, we presented the various V&V activities. The verification of parameters passes through activities of replay, testing, simulation and/or proof.

14.6.3. *Specification phase*

14.6.3.1. *ATSge description*

As shown in Figure 14.25, the specification phase has an input, planning documents (APP and other plans), system requirements, architecture and system safety requirements.

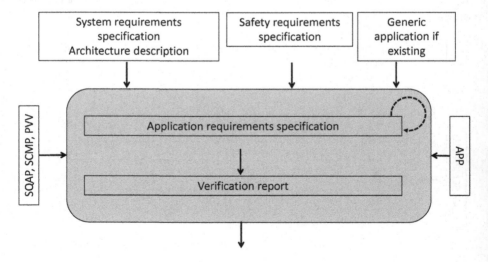

Figure 14.25. *Specification phase*

14.6.3.2. *Specifications of application requirements*

The specification phase consists of producing an application requirement specification (ARS) that needs to cover the data and generic software. For the generic software, if it is developed, it must take into account the constraints that it exports, otherwise it is necessary to describe the requirements that characterize it.

The ARS should initially contain a description of the external interfaces. Figure 14.26 allows us to view the system input interfaces (all system data and its description), annex interfaces that are existing tools, and output interfaces that are composed of the produced data for different subsystems and equipment (see Figures 14.11 and 14.12).

This vision of the process takes into account the problem of compatibility of the data produced for different subsystems. In case different data production processes were implemented (one per subsystem and/or equipment), there must be a process to ensure compatibility and consistency.

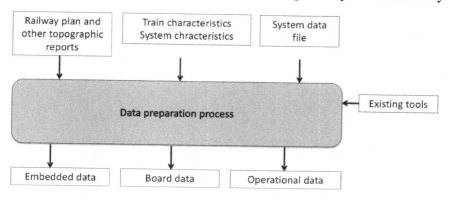

Figure 14.26. *Specification phase*

This specification should take into account the choices to be made in the APP for the data production process (see Table 14.2 and the associated discussion). We must characterize the input and output data by indicating the expected properties (functional and non-functional requirements) on that data. Note that the safety level (SIL/SSIL/DAL/ASIL/etc.) associated with the data must be identified.

The ARS must consider the separation between the generic software and the data and must therefore identify means of data protection and the interfacing principles between the parameterization data and the generic software.

For each requirement, we must identify:

– the link (traceability) with the input requirements of the phase;

– the safety attribute (yes or no);

– the verification attribute that indicates if the requirement is testable or if a specific analysis is required.

Concerning the testability of requirements, it is necessary to recall that all requirements must be verifiable and some are testable. In addition, it is necessary to check that the specification is:

– complete;

– coherent;

– comprehensive, clear and precise;

– verifiable;

– maintainable;

– traceable.

Table 14.3 shows an example of traceability between input requirements and software requirements. In the example, there appears a system requirement that is not covered; it is thus necessary to add a justification to show that nothing has been forgotten.

System requirements	Specification of software requirements
SyRS_EX_1	ARS_EX_10, ARS_EX_20
SyRS_EX_2	–
...	

Table 14.3. *Example of traceability between the system and software specifications*

Table 14.3 is not sufficient because we have to identify the software requirements that are not traceable (in aeronautics, we speak of derived requirements), so it is necessary to add a reverse traceability.

14.6.3.3. *Overall data preparation testing*

The standard does not request to develop the application overall test specification (AOTS). We recommend – in order to ensure that test cases are relevant – the realization of a specification of the whole application testing that are intended to cover all of the ARS requirements. As the only input element at this stage is the ARS, we are trying to specify black box testing (without knowledge of the realization).

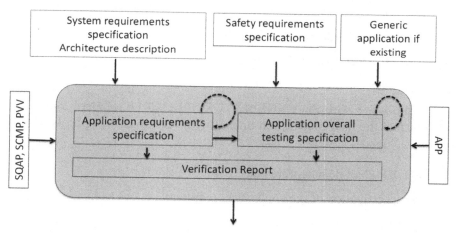

Figure 14.27. *Specification phase*

Figure 14.27 presents the stage of specification of the application after adding the AOTS. The purpose of the AOTS is to show that the parameterization process that will be realized is consistent with its requirements. Writing the AOTS can show that the requirements are testable; in fact the person in charge of producing the AOTS must carry a fine analysis of the requirements (identification of limit values for each input, identifying equivalence classes and identification of observables).

The AOTS aims to cover 100% of the requirements. For each requirement that is untestable, there must be a justification and an alternative verification activity. The AOTS must contain a traceability matrix showing that the requirements are tested and/or verified, but it must also demonstrate that each testing case is associated with a requirement.

Thus, the realization of the AOTS is a verification of the specification of the software's requirements.

14.6.3.4. Verification

Verification of the ARS (and AOTS) must cover:

– legibility requirements;

– traceability requirements;

– internal consistency requirements;

– compliance with the project quality plans;

– compliance with the CENELEC EN 50128:2011 standard taking into account that the data preparation process will rely on existing tools or tools to be developed.

The DVR shall demonstrate that:

– the specification of the application requirements has been confirmed;

– specification of the whole application testing (if performed) was verified;

– the processes defined in the APP and other plans (SQAP, SCVVP, etc.) are applied.

The verification report of the specification phase can then be formalized as the report of the review of the end-phase and follow a formal review referring to all verifications (list of input documents, lists of completed tests, review report, specific analyses, list of anomaly sheets, etc.). The formal review aims to authorize the start of the next phase (with or without reservation).

14.6.4. *Architecture phase*

14.6.4.1. *Description of architecture and design*

Once the specification of the application's requirements is realized, it is possible to set up an architecture (see Figure 14.28), but this is the architecture of the data production process.

Based on Table 14.2 and Figures 14.22 and 14.23, we must identify the tools to implement, hardware diversity (it may be necessary to run multiple tools or process) and human resources. This architecture must take into account the results of the process safety study (see section 14.6.1.5).

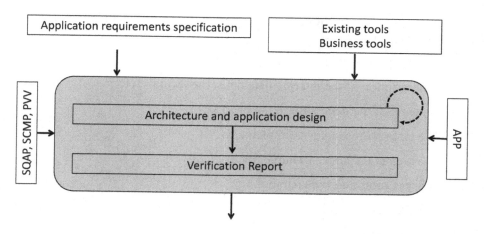

Figure 14.28. *Architecture phase*

Based on the list of tools to implement, we identify the tools to develop, trade tools and tools to reuse. For each tool, we must identify the need of qualification (Tx class) and the SSIL objective. For the tools to realize, the algorithms or transformations (see Figure 14.29) to be implemented must be specified.

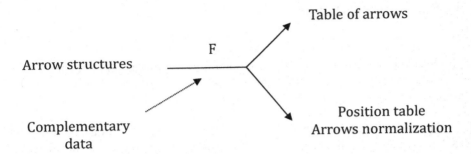

Figure 14.29. *Example of transformation*

Finally, the description of the architecture of the application (DAA) consists of:

– a description of the input data (files, etc.);

– a description of the intermediate data (file formats, etc.);

– a model of the data preparation process;

– the material resources to implement;

– the human resources to implement;

– a list of tools and for each tool:

  - the list of requirements;

  - the list of interfaces;

  - Tx class and SSIL objectives;

  - algorithms to implement;

– one or more traceability matrices.

One of the important topics at this stage concerns the production of intermediate files and their control (which configuration management, which protection, etc.).

14.6.4.2. *Integration testing*

The 2011 version of the CENELEC EN 50128 standard does not provide the preparation of integration tests. Given the complexity of the data preparation process (several tools, various machines and several people involved), it is preferable to provide software/software and software/hardware integration testing. The complete architecture phase is given in Figure 14.30.

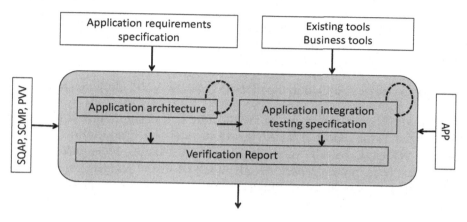

Figure 14.30. *Architecture phase with the integration tests*

Software/software integration tests aim to ensure that the exchanges between the tools work properly (correct file name, correct format, good data accuracy, effective protection of files, etc.). Software/hardware integration tests are intended to demonstrate that the software works properly (proper functioning, no memory over-consumption, acceptable memory consumption and running time, etc.).

It is possible to realize two different documents or a single document; we will discuss the application integration tests specification (AITS). The purpose of the AITS is to show that the software/software and software/hardware interfaces are correct.

Since the only input elements at this point of the project are description documents, we are trying to specify black box testing (without knowledge of the realization).Thus, the realization of the AITS is a verification of the DAA.

14.6.4.3. *Verification report*

As already indicated, the CENELEC EN 50128:2011 standard identifies a verification report for the end of each phase. This verification report shall demonstrate that:

– the specification of the application's architecture has been verified;

– the specification of application integration tests (if performed) was verified;

– the processes defined in the plans (SQAP, SCVVP, etc.) are applied.

The verification report of the architecture and design phase can then be formalized as the report of the review of the end-phase, and follow a formal review referring to all verifications (list of input documents, list of completed tests, review report, specific analysis, list of anomaly sheets, etc.). The formal review aims to authorize the start of the next phase (with or without reservation).

14.6.5. *Data production*

14.6.5.1. *Design of algorithms*

With a data architecture process and algorithms, it is possible to implement the data production process. Figure 14.31 recalls that the data production process must take into account two aspects:

– data production;

– the production of the final executable (data + generic software).

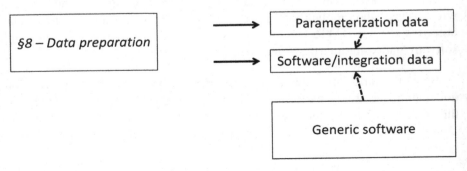

Figure 14.31. *Relationship between the two realization processes*

Concerning the production of data, clause 8.4.4.1 specifies that diagrammatic languages are recommended to produce the data. There is a link on Table A.16 of the CENELEC EN 50128:2011 standard (see Table 14.4). This recommendation complements lines 1 and 2 of Table A.11 that mention modeling based on tables and specific languages.

Measure	SSIL0	SSIL1 SSIL2	SSIL3 SSIL4
1. Functional diagram	R	R	R
2. Function sequential graph	–	HR	HR
3. Contact diagrams	R	R	R
4. Graphical states	R	HR	HR

Table 14.4. *Table A.16 of the CENELEC EN 50128:2011 standard*

Concerning Table 14.4, lines 1–3 are directly linked to the standard part 3 of the IEC 61131:2003 standard[7] [IEC 03]. Line 4 which refers to graphical states should read "States/transitions graph" in a broad sense (see Figure 14.18). Remember that this version of the standard indicates that it is possible to use languages that are not cited after demonstration of their adequacy for the application.

In the end, the standard recommends using a graphical language close to the field (keeping the specifics of signaling, for example, to facilitate the verification by experts in the field) to describe data and to describe transformations to realize in order to produce the application data.

At this level, the CENELEC EN 50128:2011 is not very specific about the documentation to realize. Existing tools (COTS, tools of the trade, reused tools) can be implemented, the tools may have been realized (see clause 8.4.7) and a specific coding of data may have been implemented. If we want to specify and perform tests (see clauses 8.4.4.2, 8.4.4.3, etc.), it is necessary to have design documents that will ensure the software's maintenance. It therefore seems necessary to have at least one design document. We therefore recommend producing detailed design documents for each tool or algorithm to code.

---

7 The IEC 61131 standard [IEC 03] introduces the syntax and semantics of the programming languages of programmable automatons.

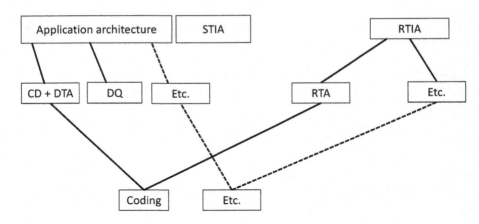

Figure 14.32. *Realization of the data production process*

Figure 14.32 shows that from the document describing the architecture, it is possible to identify tools to re-use (COTS, commercial tools or existing tools) and the tools qualification report shall demonstrate the adequacy of the tool to the needs. If a development is necessary, a detailed design document and associated tests (see the following section) are to be produced.

14.6.5.2. *Algorithm testing*

The 2011 version of the standard offers many improvements to process the production of data but some points still need to be clarified, such as algorithms and design testing. The clauses 8.4.4.2 and 8.4.4.3 address the relationship of the application testing while the application tests specification (ATS) is defined only later (clauses 8.4.4.5 and 8.4.4.6).

The ATS should show that the data and/or algorithms comply with the requirements and architecture. It is therefore best to have a design document that identifies the need and that can be useful to coding and production of testing.

In the previous sections, we have introduced comprehensive testing and integration testing; at this level, it would be preferable to introduce testing of algorithms and/or data that is intended to show that the functionalities are present in the tools used and/or the developed algorithms are working properly. The ATS would be more of the type of component or module testing. The realization of the ATS is therefore a verification of the design documents (if they exist).

Once the algorithms or data are testable, we must perform the tests described in the ATS and write a report on the application's tests (ATR), which documents the test results (version, date, name of tester, etc.).

To conclude this section, we can indicate that the set consisting of the AOTS, AITS and ATS can meet clause 8.4.4.5 and that the set composed of the AOTR, AITR and ATR can meet clause 8.4.4.2.

14.6.5.3. *Data verification*

Clause 8.4.4.4 introduces a specific verification report for the preparation of an application (application preparation verification report [APVR]). The verification of algorithms and/or data is done through the replay activity consisting of verifying (see Figure 14.33):

– the existence of the data manipulated by the development process;

– the existence of the data manipulated by the software;

– the existence and correctness of the generation process;

– traceability of requirements applies to data.

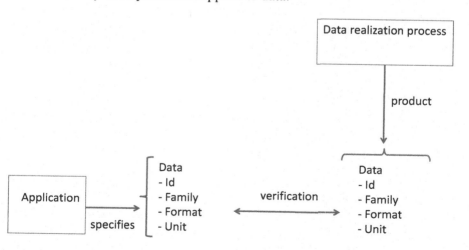

Figure 14.33. *Data compatibility*

The algorithm and/or data verification activities should allow to show that the data are correct and complete. These activities must be documented in the APVR. These verifications can be introduced into the process (double execution, specific verification tool, tool of proof of ownership, etc.) or be designed as specific checks or tests.

14.6.5.4. *Verification of the activity*

As already mentioned, the activity must be verified, a DVR must be produced where the overall DVR must be updated, and checks must provide evidence that:

– the processes defined in the APP and other plans (SQAP, SCVVP, etc.) are applied;

– the design of algorithms and/or data has been verified;

– the specification of algorithm tests (if performed) has been verified (e.g. with an analysis of the coverage of requirements);

– the report of the algorithm tests (if realized) has been verified;

– the verification of data (APVR) has been verified.

The report of the review of the end-phase is formalized and a formal review referring to all verifications is followed (list of input documents, lists of completed checks, review report, specific analysis, list of anomaly sheets, etc.). The formal review aims to authorize the start of the next phase (with or without reservation).

14.6.5.5. *Synthesis*

The design phase of algorithms and data is quite complex, as shown in Figure 14.33. The CENELEC EN 50128:2011 standard remains rather ambiguous on the activities to implement effectively.

Figure 14.34 contains only the application's tests (related to algorithms and/or data), but if we implement integration testing (AITS) and overall testing (AOTS), it is during this phase that we must incorporate (see Figure 14.31) the tools to perform the data production process, and it is in this phase that we must show that the process meets the requirements of the specification. The AITR and AOTR are to be produced and verified during this phase.

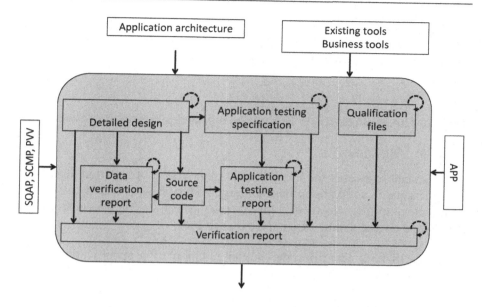

Figure 14.34. *Design phase of data and algorithms*

As part of a certifiable application, it is necessary to be able to replay the tests identically; we must therefore document the testing realization process, manage configuration input data and results as well as all the necessary elements necessary for the implementation of testing.

The structure of the test reports (ATR, AITR and AOTR) are structured as follows:

– identification of the input elements;

– identification of applicable plans (SQAP, etc.);

– methods used: people, tools, environment, etc.;

– analyzed version;

– list of test cases;

– demonstration of the achievement of objectives;

– assessment of the problems identified;

– conclusion on the correction of the version.

The assessment of identified problems requires that for each detected failure an anomaly sheet is formed. This anomaly sheet must describe the identified problem and the activities and the factors that enabled its implementation.

14.6.6. *The application's integration and acceptance of testing*

14.6.6.1. *Activities*

This stage concerns the integration of data and/or application algorithms with the generic software on its final target. This phase is usually associated with factory testing. However, other techniques can be implemented such as exhaustive on-site testing (long and expensive).

Clause 8.4.5.2 identifies the implementation of a specification of the application tests that shall demonstrate:

– the correct integration of data and/or application algorithms with the generic software on its final target;

– the correct integration of data and/or application algorithms with the full installation.

It is a negative point that the standard identifies the document as being the same as that identified in the data production phase (in the previous section of this chapter). We recommend to define a specific test document, named installation test specification (ITS). One of the important inputs for the ITS is related to constraints exported by the generic software and the data process.

The report of the installation tests (ITR) is to be realized at the end of the performance tests. It should identify what has been tested, by whom, when and the results.

14.6.6.2. *Verification of the activity*

As already mentioned, the activity must be verified, a DVR must be produced where the overall DVR must be updated, and checks must provide evidence that:

– the processes defined in the APP and other plans (SQAP, SCVVP, etc.) are applied;

– the ITS was verified (e.g. with an analysis of the coverage of requirements);

– the ITR has been verified.

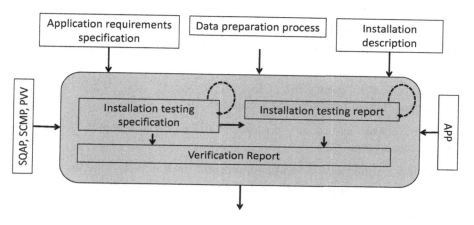

Figure 14.35. *Data and algorithm design phase*

14.6.6.3. *Synthesis*

Figure 14.35 shows the complete stage as recommended. We can highlight that verification is a very important part of the complete data preparation process.

14.6.7. *Validation and evaluation of the application*

Clause 8.4.6 recommends implementing verification activities during each phase. We have included this recommendation within each phase that we presented (see the dotted arrows that are verifications); there is nothing more to realize.

14.6.8. *Procedures and application preparation tools*

14.6.8.1. *Perimeter*

Clause 8.4.7 of the standard covers several topics and states that:

– the development of specific tools must comply with the CENELEC EN 50128: 2011 standard;

– the need to validate and evaluate the compilation process taking into account the data and/or algorithms (a compilation channel dedicated may be required);

– clauses 9.1 (concerning the deployment) and 9.2 (concerning maintenance) must be taken into account;

– the software assurance – as already discussed in Chapter 5 – must be taken into account;

– that the application's verification report must demonstrate the coverage of exported constraints by both the generic software and the data.

The finalization of the data production process and associated activities must be formalized by the production of a software version sheet (SVS). This SVS must identify the configuration of the implemented tools, document configuration and must contain the exported constraints and/or usage limitations.

14.6.8.2. *Synthesis*

Clause 8.4.7 does not define new objectives and reinforces what we mentioned in Chapter 2, that the process to implement for realizing the data preparation process must comply with ISO 9001:2015. The software's maintenance and deployment are presented in the context of Chapters 9 and 10.

14.6.9. *Development of the generic software*

We presented the needs in the context of the definition of the realization process and the writing of the APP in section 14.5.2.2.

There are three important points:

– it is necessary to demonstrate that the overall tests of the generic software cover all the relevant data configurations. In case all the combinations have not been tested, the limits of use must be identified;

– as part of software maintenance, we will need to demonstrate that any change impacting the generic software (or configuration data) has been the object of an impact assessment in order to verify if the configuration data (or generic software) are impacted or not;

– it is necessary to demonstrate that the generic software and configuration data are compatible.

The realization of generic software will result in an SVS. In section 14.7.8.1, we identified the existence of the SVS for the data production process. For a given installation, we will therefore need to produce an SVS for the installation, which will describe:

– the SVS of the generic software used;

– the SVS of the data production process;

– the configuration of the input data used.

14.7. Conclusion

The CENELEC EN 50128:2011 standard – and its international version the IEC 62279:2014 – allows the treatment of two aspects: the development of a generic software application (see section 7 of the standard) and the development of a process to parameterize a generic application (see section 8).

In Volume 3 [BOU 17a], we will present the process of developing a generic software application. This chapter described the data production process. The data production process is based on the control of the software quality assurance and the development and/or the reuse of tools. The development of a tool can either follow a standard (DO 178, ISO 26262, and CENELEC EN 50128:2011) or be associated with a qualification (see Chapter 13).

The implementation of a data preparation process will require the qualification of associated tools; they will be classified as T3[8] or T2[9].

We presented the principles of data preparation, constraints and recommendations. Indeed, although section **8** of the CENELEC EN 50128:2011 standard (see also section **8** of the IEC 62279 [IEC 14]) is a real progress, it is still not sufficient to realize a process. This is due to the complexity of the parameterization process and the large number of possibilities.

Note that for other fields, there is an introduction of parameters, but the standards do not introduce associated recommendations on the production process of these parameters.

---

8 Class T3 is dedicated to tools where a fault could have an effect on the final executable. This class concerns compilators, code generators, etc.

9 Class T2 is dedicated to tools where a fault could have an effect on verification or validation results. This class contains coding rules verification tools, metrics measurement tools, code static analysis tools, test execution management tools, etc.

Audit

15.1. Introduction

The control of quality involves the control of product quality, and to do this, it is possible to conduct one or more audits to verify the correct application of business processes.

This chapter aims to introduce the concept of audit and associated processes. This is a support process that will be very useful to control the quality of the product.

15.2. Audit

The audit must be associated with a process that is defined through several phases:

– *audit preparation*: we must define the purpose of the audit (quality, configuration, etc.) and scope (enterprise, department, service, project, team, activity). From there, it is possible to identify the input elements required to perform the audit (quality plan, etc.);

– *audit planification*: following the preparation stage, it is necessary to produce an audit plan that will identify the date, scope, audit program (themes, expected people, timing, etc.), etc.;

– *performing the audit*: based on the audit plan that was established in the previous phase, the audit is performed. During the audit, elements are collected in order to verify the audit objectives;

– *formalization of audit results*: we must formalize the audit results as an audit report to take into consideration the evidence presented during the audit and the list of identified non-conformities or observations;

– *follow-up of observations*: observations and non-conformities of the audit are to be monitored. Actions should be identified and implemented.

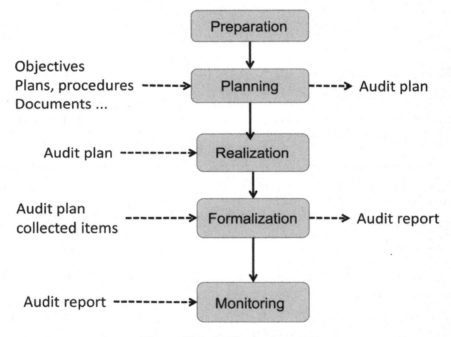

Figure 15.1. *Audit management*

Figure 15.1 allows us to view the audit process as a whole. This process is quite simple but is essential in controlling the quality of a product.

15.3. Conclusion

The quality audit is a support process that can be implemented to control different points as follows:

– control of the quality reference: QAM, procedure, standard plan, etc.;

– adequate application of the quality reference;

– quality of the documentation;

– the code's quality;

– control of the product's configuration.

Conclusions and Perspectives

Volume 1 [BOU 16] of this series gave us an opportunity to present the link that must be established between system and software applications through architectural stages. It is indeed necessary to ensure that the software application works correctly in an environment that is generally quite complex. In the context of complex systems such as transportation, energy and production, safety, reliability and maintainability of the system depend directly on the software application. Also, Volume 1 gave us the opportunity to present the process of the realization of a software application taking into account all the constraints related to a complex and certifiable safe system.

Volume 2, the present book, allowed for the identification and description of the support processes that are needed to be implemented in order to build a certifiable application. Among these, we find quality assurance, configuration management, change management, definition of versions, archiving, verification and validation, data preparation, management and qualification of tools and audits. These processes are essential but are generally poorly applied.

Therefore, it is necessary to build a quality management system that includes the entire support process by defining procedures, standard plans, a quality assurance manual, guides and all the elements to facilitate the realization of a new project.

Glossary

ACA:	Architecture and Conception of the Application
ACATS:	ADA Conformity Assessment Test Suite
AdL:	Software Architect
ADTR:	Application Design Testing Report
AITR:	Application Integration Testing Report
AITS:	Application Integration Testing Specification
AOTR:	Overall Application Testing Report
AOTS:	Application Overall Test Specification
AP:	Automatic Pilot
APP:	Application Preparation Plan
APVR:	Application Preparation Verification Report
ARS:	Application Requirements Specifications
ASA:	Automata and Structured Analysis
ASIL:	Automotive SIL
ASN[1]:	Nuclear Safety Authority
ASR:	ASsessoR
ASTE:	Automation System of Train Exploitation
ATO:	Automatic Train Operation
ATR:	Application Testing Report

---

1 www.asn.fr

ATS:	Application Tests Specification
BDD:	Binary Decision Diagram
CCB:	Change Control Board
CCC:	Change Control Committee
CCR:	Critcal Code Review
CD:	Compact Disk
CEI:	Electrotechnical International Commission
CENELEC[2]:	European Committee for Electrotechnical Standardization
CI:	Configuration Item
CM:	Configuration Management
CMM:	Configuration Management Manager
CMMi:	Capability Maturity Model for integration
CMP:	Configuration Management Plan
COTS:	Commercial Off-the-Shelf
CSP:	Coded Safety Processor
CT:	Component Tests
CV:	Curriculum Vitae
DAA:	Description of the Application's Architecture
DAL:	Design Assurance Level
DES:	Designer
DM:	Dependability Manager
DR:	Deployement Register
DVD:	Digital Versatile Disc
DVR:	Data Verification Report
E/E/PE:	Electrical/Electronic/Programmable Electronic
EMC:	Electromagnetic Compatibility
ET:	Element Testing
FDMS:	*Fiabilité, Disponibilité, Maintenabilité et Sécurité*
FMEA:	Failure Modes and Effects Analysis

---

2 See the website: www.cenelec.eu/

FMECA:	Failure Modes and Effects Criticality Analysis
FPGA:	Field Programmable Gate Arrays
GE:	*Gestionnaire des Exigences*
GL:	Glossary
GPS:	Global Positioning System
GT:	General Testing
HR:	Highly Recommended
IEC[3]:	International Electro-technical Commission
IMP:	Implementer
INT:	Integrator
ISA:	Independent Safety Assessor
ISO[4]:	International Organization for Standardization
IT:	Integration Test
ITR:	Installation Testing Report
ITS:	Installation Tests Specification
KP:	Kilometer Point
M:	Mandatory
MAGGALY:	*Métro à Grand Gabarit de l'Agglomération de Lyon*
METEOR:	*MÉTro-Est-Ouest-Rapide*
MU:	Monitoring Unit
NATO:	North Atlantic Treaty Organization
nOOm:	n out of m
OATS:	Overall ApplicationTest Specification
OCC:	Operating Control Center
OMG:	Object Management Group[5]
OS:	Operating system
OST:	Overall Software Tests

---

3 See: http://www.iec.ch/
4 See: http://www.iso.org/iso/home.htm
5 See: http://www.omg.org/

OT:	Overall Test
PM:	Project Manager
PSC:	Secure Coded Processor
QA:	Quality Assurance
QAM:	Quality Assurance Manual
QAP:	Quality Assurance Plan
QM:	Quality Manager
QMS:	Quality Management System
QR:	Qualification Report
QUA:	Quality Engineer
R:	Recommended
RAMS:	Reliability, Availability, Maintainability and Safety
RDL:	Residual Defect List
REQ:	Requirement
RQM:	Requirements Manager
S/H:	Software/Hardware
S/H IT:	Software/Hardware Integration Testing
S/S:	Software/Software
S/S IT:	Software/Software Integration Testing
SA:	Software Architect
SACEM:	Driving and Maintenance Assistance System
SADT:	Structured Analysis and Design Technic
SAET:	System of Automatization of Train Operations
SAP:	Safety Assurance Plan
SC:	Safety Case
SCMP:	Software Configuration Management Plan
SDM:	Software Application Deployment Manual
SDP:	Software Development Plan
SDR:	Software Application Deployment Register
SD-VR:	Software Application Deployment – Verification Report

SE:	Safety Engineer
SEEA:	Software Error Effects Analysis
SIL:	Safety Integrity Level
SM:	Safety Manager
SMP:	Software Maintenance Plan
SPICE:	Software Process Improvement and Capability Determination
SPIN:	Separation and Incineration in Reactor
SQAP:	Software Quality Assurance Plan
SSIL:	Software Safety Integrity Level
ST:	Set Tests
STCA:	Specification of Application Design Tests
SVaP:	Software Validation Plan
SVeP:	Software Verification Plan
SVS:	Software Application Version Sheet
SVS:	Software Version Sheet
SwCMP:	Software Configuration Management Plan
SwRS:	Software Requirement Specification
SwS-VR:	Software Specification - Verification Report
SVVP:	Software Verification and Validation Plan
SyRS:	System Requirement Specification
SyAD:	System Architecture Description
TC:	Track Circuit
TCL:	Tool Confidence Level
TD:	Tool Error Detection
TI:	Tool Impact
TM:	Tools Manager
TQL:	Tool Qualification Level
TQR:	Tools Qualification Report
TST:	Tester

TVR:	Tools Validation Report
Tx:	Tool Qualitfication Objective: T1, T2 or T3.
UML:	Unified Modeling Language
UT:	Unit Test
V&V:	Verification and Validation
VAL:	Valider
VAL:	Light Autonomous Vehicle
VER:	Verifier
VOB:	Versioned Object Base
VT:	Validation Test
VVP:	Verification and Validation Plan

Bibliography

[ABR 96] ABRIAL Jr., *The B Book – Assigning Programs to Meanings*, Cambridge University Press, 1996.

[ADA 01] ADA RESOURCE ASSOCIATION, "Operating procedures for Ada conformity assessments", Version 3.0, Ada Resource Association, available at www.ada-auth.org/procs/3.0/ACAP30.pdf, 2001.

[ANS 83] ANSI, Programming Language Ada, Standard ANSI/MIL-STD-1815A-1983, 1983.

[ARI 92], ARINC, Software considerations in airborne systems and equipment certification, DO 178B Standard l'EUROCAE, no. ED12, B, 1992.

[BAI 08] BAIER C., KATOEN J.P., *Principles of Model Checking*, MIT Press, 2008.

[BAR 14] BARNES J., *Programming in Ada 2012*, Cambridge University Press, 2014.

[BAU 11] BAUFRETON P., BLANQUART J.P., BOULANGER J.L. *et al.*, "Comparaison de normes de sécurité–innocuité de plusieurs domaines industriels", *Revue REE*, vol. 2, 2011.

[BEH 96] BEHM P., "Formal development of safety critical software of METEOR", *First B Conference*, Nantes, France, November, pp. 24–26, 1996.

[BOE 88] BOEHM B.W, "A spiral model of software development and enhancement", *IEEE Computer*, vol. 21, pp. 61–72, 1988.

[BOU 99] BOULANGER J.L., DELEBARRE V., NATKIN S., "METEOR: validation of specification by formal model", *Revue RTS*, vol. 63, pp. 47–62, 1999.

[BOU 00] BOULANGER J.L., GALLARDO M., "Processus de validation basée sur la notion de propriété", *LamnbdaMu*, 2000.

[BOU 03] BOULANGER J.L., "Validation of the data linked to safety", *Qualita, Quality and Dependability (RAMS)*, Nancy, France, 19–21 March 2003

[BOU 06] BOULANGER J.L., Expression and validation of logical and physical safety properties for critical computer systems, Thesis, University of Technology of Compiègne, 2006.

[BOU 07a] BOULANGER J.L., "Art state of the validation of data in the railway field", *Revue REE*, pp. 25–31, March, 2007.

[BOU 07b] BOULANGER J.L., BON P., "BRAIL: d'UML à la méthode B pour modéliser un passage à niveau", *Revue RTS*, vol. 95, pp. 147–172, 2007.

[BOU 08] BOULANGER J.L., "RT3–TUCS: how to build a certifiable and safety critical railway application", *17th International Conference on Software Engineering and Data Engineering (SEDE)*, Los Angeles, pp. 182–187, 2008.

[BOU 09a] BOULANGER J.L., *Sécurisation des Architectures Informatiques – Exemples Concrets*, Hermes Science-Lavoisier, Paris, 2009.

[BOU 09b] BOULANGER J.L., IDANI A., PHILIPPE L., "Linking paradigms in safety critical systems", *Revue ICSA*, 2009.

[BOU 09c] BOULANGER J.L., "Le domaine ferroviaire, les produits et la certification", Ecole des mines de Nantes, 2009.

[BOU 10] BOULANGER J.L., (ed.) *Safety of Computer Architectures*, ISTE Ltd, London and John Wiley & Sons, New York, 2010.

[BOU 11a] BOULANGER J.L. (ed.), *Sécurisation des architectures informatiques industrielles*, Hermès Science-Lavoisier, Paris, 2011.

[BOU 11b] BOULANGER J.L. (ed), *Static Analysis of Software*, ISTE Ltd, London and John Wiley and Sons, 2011.

[BOU 11c] BOULANGER J.L. (ed), *Techniques industrielles de modélisation formelle pour le transport*, Hermes Science-Lavoisier, Paris, 2011.

[BOU 14a] BOULANGER J.L., *Industrial Implementation of Formal Techniques – Method B*, Hermes, Paris, 2014.

[BOU 14b] BOULANGER J.L., BADREAU S., *Formal Methods Applied to Industrial Complex Systems: Implementation of the B Method*, ISTE Ltd, London and John Wiley & Sons, New York, 2014.

[BOU 16] BOULANGER J.L., *Certifiable Software Applications 1*, ISTE Press, London and Elsevier, Oxford, 2016.

[BOU 17a] BOULANGER J.L., *Certifiable Software Applications 3*, ISTE Press, London and Elsevier, Oxford, forthcoming, 2017.

[BOU 17b] BOULANGER J.L., *Certifiable Software Applications 4*, ISTE Press, London and Elsevier, Oxford, forthcoming, 2017.

[CEN 00] CENELEC, Railway applications; specification and demonstration of reliability, NF EN 50126, CENELEC, 2000.

[CEN 01] CENELEC, Railway applications: signalling system, telecommunications and processing – Software for command system and railway protection, NF EN 50128, July 2001.

[CEN 03] CENELEC, Applications ferroviaires: systèmes de signalisation, de télécommunications et de traitement systèmes électroniques de sécurité pour la signalization, NF EN 50129, 2003.

[CEN 07] CENELEC, Railway applications: communication, signalling and processing systems – application guide, EN 50129, May, 2007.

[CEN 11a] CENELEC, Railway applications: signalling system, telecommunications and processing – software for control and train protection system, NF EN 50128, 2011.

[CEN 11b] CENELEC Railway applications: communications, signaling and processing systems – Software for railway control and protection systems, EN 50128, January, 2011.

[CEN 12] CENELEC, Railway applications: specification and demonstration of reliability, NF EN 50126, 2012.

[CHA 96] CHAUMETTE A.M., LE FEVRE L., "Automation system of the exploitation of trains in the line METEOR", *REE*, 1996.

[CHI 94] CHIDAMBER S.R., KEMERER C.F., "A metric suite for object oriented design", *IEEE Transactions on Software Engineering*, vol. 20, pp. 476–493, 1994.

[COU 00] COUSOT P., "Interprétation abstraite", available at: www.di.ens. fr/~cousot/COUSOTpapers/TSI00.shtml, 2000.

[DEL 99] DELEBARRE V., GALLARDO M., JUPPEAUX E. *et al.*, "Validation des constantes de sécurité du pilote automatique de METEOR", *ICSARS'99*, CNAM, Paris, 1999.

[DOR 08] DORMOY F.X., "Scade 6 a model based solution for safety critical software development", *Embedded Real-Time Systems Conference*, 2008.

[GAL 08] GALLARDO M., BOULANGER J.L., "Poste de manœuvre à enclenchement informatique: démonstration de la sécurité", *Conférence Internationale Francophone d'Automatique, Bucarest*, Roumania, 2008.

[GAR 94] GARIN H., *AMDEC – AMDE – AEEL –The Essence of the Method*, AFNOR, 1994.

[GEO 90] GEORGES J.P., "Principes et fonctionnement du Système d'Aide à la Conduite, à l'Exploitation et à la Maintenance (SACEM). Application à la ligne A du RER", *Revue Générale des Chemins de Fer*, vol. 6, 1990.

[GRA 93] GRAHAM G., *Software Inspection*, Addison Wesley, 1993.

[HAB 91] HABRIAS H., *The Software Measurement*, 2nd ed., Teknea, 1991.

[HOA 69] HOARE C.A.R., "An axiomatic basis for computer programming", *Communications of the ACM*, vol. 12, no. 10, pp. 576–580, 1969.

[IDA 06] IDANI A., B/UML: mise en relation de spécifications B et de descriptions UML pour l'aide à la validation externe de développements formels en B, PhD thesis, Joseph Fourier-Grenoble 1 University, 2006.

[IDA 07a] IDANI A., BOULANGER J.L., PHILIPPE L., "A generic process and its tool support towards combining UML and B for safety critical systems", *CAINE*, San Francisco, 2007.

[IDA 07b] IDANI A., OKASA OSSAMI D.D., BOULANGER J.L., "Commandments of UML for safety", *2nd International Conference on Software Engineering Advances*, 2007.

[IDA 09] IDANI A., BOULANGER J.L., PHILIPPE L., "Linking paradigms in safety critical systems", *Revue ICSA*, 2009.

[IEC 98] IEC, Functional safety of safety-related programmable electronic electrical systems, *IEC 67508*, 1998.

[IEC 00] IEC, Functional safety of programmable electronic electrical systems related to standard, *IEC 617508*, 2000.

[IEC 03] IEC, Automates programmables – Partie 3: Langages de programmation, CEI 61131–3:2003, 2003.

[IEC 06] IEC, Nuclear power plants – instrumentation and command-controls important for safety. Software aspects of programmed systems performing the functions of categories A, IEC 60880, 2006.

[IEC 08] IEC, Functional safety of safety-related programmable electronic electrical systems, IEC 61508, 2008.

[IEC 10] IEC, Sécurité fonctionnelle des systèmes électriques électroniques programmables relatifs à la sécurité, IEC 61508, 2010.

[IEC 11] IEC, Railway applications – communication, signaling and processing systems – software for railway control and protection systems, IEC 62279, 2011.

[IEC 14] IEC, Railway applications – communication, signaling and processing systems – software for railway control and protection systems, IEC 62279, 2014.

[IEC 15] IEC, Sécurité fonctionnelle des systèmes électriques électroniques programmables relatifs à la sécurité, Norme internationale, IEC 61508, 2015.

[ISO 85] ISO, Processing of information – vocabulary of software quality, ISO Z61-102, 1985.

[ISO 91] ISO, Information technology – software product evaluation – quality characteristics and guidelines for their use, ISO 9126, 1991.

[ISO 95] ISO, Information technology – programming languages – Ada, ISO 8652, 1995.

[ISO 99a] ISO, ISO Standard, Technical report, available at http://www.open-std.org/jtc1/sc22/wg14/www/docs/n1124.pdf, 1999.

[ISO 99b] ISO, Information technology – programming languages – Ada: conformity assessment of a language processor, ISO ICE 18009, 1999

[ISO 00] ISO, Systems of quality management – essential principles and Vocabulary, ISO 9000, 2000.

[ISO 03] ISO, Quality management systems – guidelines for configuration management, ISO 10007:2003, 2003.

[ISO 04a] ISO, Ingénierie du logiciel – Lignes directrices pour l'application de l'ISO 9001:2000 aux logiciels informatiques, ISO/IEC 90003:2004, 2004.

[ISO 04b] ISO, Information technology – process assessment, ISO, plusieurs parties publiées entre, ISO/IEC 15504-x, 2004/2011.

[ISO 04c] ISO, Information technology – software product evaluation – quality characteristics and guidelines for their use, ISO9126:2004, 2004.

[ISO 04d] ISO, Information technology – process assessment – part 4: guidance on use for process improvement and process capability determination, initially known by the name of SPICE (Software Process Improvement and Capability determination), ISO/CEI 15504, 2004.

[ISO 04e] ISO, Software engineering – guidelines for the application of ISO 9001:2000 to Computer Software, ISO 90003, 2004

[ISO 11] ISO, Road vehicles – functional safety, ISO 26262, 2011.

[ISO 14] ISO, Ingénierie du logiciel – exigences de qualité du produit logiciel et évaluation (SQuaRE) – Guide de SQuaRE, ISO 25000, 2014.

[ISO 15a] ISO, Systèmes de management de la qualité – exigence, ISO 9001, 2015.

[ISO 15b] ISO, Quality Management Systems – requirement, ISO 9001, 2015.

[JON 90] JONES C.B., *Systematic Software Development Using VDM*, 2nd ed., Prentice Hall International, 1990.

[LIS 90] LISSANDRE M., *Maîtriser SADT*, Armand Colin, 1990.

[MAI 93] MAIRE A., "Presentation of the system MAGGALY", *International Symposium on Technological Innovation in Guided Transport*, (ITIG'93), Lille, 1993.

[MAM 01] MAMMAR A., LALEAU R., "An automatic generation of B-specification from well-defined UML notations for database applications", *CNAM*, Paris, 2001.

[MAR 01] MARCANO R., LEVY N., "Transformation d'annotations OCL en expressions B", *Journées Approches Formelles dans L'Assistance au Développement de Logiciels AFADL*, 2001.

[MAR 04] MARCANO R., COLIN S., MARIANO G., "A formal framework for uml modelling with timed constraint: Application to railway control system", *Specification Validation of UML models for Real Time and Embedded Systems SVERTS*, 2004.

[MAT 98] MATRA, RATP, "Birth of a subway. On the new line 14, the METEOR trains come in", *The Life of Rail & Transport*, no. 1076, Hors-série, 1998.

[MIS 98] MISRA, "Guidelines for the use of the C language in vehicle based software", *Motor Industry Research Association, MISRA-C*, April 1998.

[MIS 04] MISRA, "Guidelines for the use of the C language in critical systems", *Motor Industry Research Association MISRA-C*, 2004.

[MIS 08] MISRA, "Guidelines for the use of the C++ language in critical systems", *Motor Industry Research Association MISRA-C*, 2008.

[MON 00] MONIN J.F., *Understanding Formal Methods*, Hermes Science, Paris, 2000.

[MYE 79] MYERS V, *The Art of Software Testing*, John Wiley & Sons, 1979

[NAU 69] NAUR, R. (eds), Software engineering: a report on a conference sponsored by NATO Science Committee, NATO, 1969

[NET 10] NET, La fiabilité des CD, DVD et disques durs remise en cause, 2010.

[NF 90] NF, Fixed installations and rail rolling material, informatics, dependability of software – methods suitable for analyses of safety software, NF-71–013, December 1990.

[OFT 97] OFTA, "Application of formal techniques to the software", Arago 20, 1997

[OMG 11] OMG, Unified Modeling Language: Infrastructure, 2011.

[OMG 06a] OMG, Unified Modeling Language: Superstructure, Version 2.1, OMG Ptc Document/06-01-02, 2006.

[OMG 06b] OMG, Unified Modeling Language: Infrastructure, Version 2.0, OMG Formal Document/05-07-05, 2006.

[ROQ 07] ROQUES P., *UML 2 – Modéliser une application Web*, Eyrolles, Paris, 2007.

[RTA 11] RTA DO 330, Software tools qualification consideration, Version C, RTA, 2011.

[RTC 92] RTCA DO-178B/ED-12B, Software considerations in airborne systems and equipment certification, RTCA, 1992.

[RTC 11] RTCA DO 178 :C, Software consideration in airborne systems and equipment certification, Version C, RTCA, 2011.

[SOM 07] SOMMERVILLE I., "Software engineering", Version 8, 2007.

[SPI 89] SPIVEY J.M., *The Z Notation – A Reference Manual*, Prentice Hall International, 1989.

[THI 86] THIREAU P., "Méthodologie d'Analyse des Effets des Erreurs Logiciel (AEEL) appliquée à l'étude d'un logiciel de haute sécurité", *5th International Conference on Reliability and Maintainability*, Biarritz, France, 1986.

[VIL 88] VILLEMEUR A., *Functioning Safety of Industrial Systems,* Eyrolles, Paris, 1988.

[WAE 95] WAESELYNCK H., BOULANGER J.L., "The role of testing in the b formal development process", *ISSRE'95,* Toulouse, October, pp. 25–27, 1995.

[WAT 96] WATSON A.H., MCCABE T.J., "Structured testing – a methodology using the cyclomatic complexity metric", *Report NIST,* pp. 500–235, 1996.

[XAN 99] XANTHAKIS S., RÉGNIER P., KARAPOULIOS C., *Software Test,* Hermes Science, Paris, 1999.

Index

Printed in the United States
By Bookmasters